TEACHING OF THE TWELVE APOSTLES TO THE GENTILES

ESSAYS IN EARLY CHURCH LITERATURE: NO. 01

BRENT S. WALTERS

Curator, Ante-Nicene Archive
Dean, College of Early Christian Studies

CENTRE FOR EARLY CHRISTIAN STUDIES

2018

This volume is dedicated to David John Bird.

We have but faith: we cannot know;
For knowledge is of things we see
And yet we trust it comes from thee,
A beam in darkness: let it grow.

Tennyson, *In Memoriam 21-24*

FOREWORD

Secluded beneath tall, feeble buildings and nestled in a meager, modest township stood a renowned monastery in a section of Constantinople called Phanar. Among the five hundred manuscripts in the library was a tome, later identified as the Jerusalem Codex, that remained hidden for over eight hundred years. One of its treasures was *The Teaching of the Twelve Apostles*, a work counted among the earliest writings of the church. The scholar who found it, Philotheos Bryennios, prepared its first printed edition that he composed in scholastic Greek and distributed to libraries throughout the West. As a result, it drew immediate attention and became an historical phenomenon in academic circles. For this reason, the manual has become indispensable reading for those intent on recapturing the essence of the faith.

Bryennios lived in a narrow, wooden, unpainted, four-story house located a few steps away from the monastery and opposite the entrance to the patriarchal church. The prelate was among the most educated in the Orthodox Church and was well read in classical and patristic literature. He first spotted the *Teaching* in 1873, and while lost for 1,500 years, this brief treatise purports to contain authentic apostolic instruction. The folio was comprised of one hundred and twenty pages of a small octavo codex and contained prominent works from the first century, including the epistles of Clement, Ignatius, and Barnabas, as well as the *Teaching*. It is a superb example of what was considered essential doctrine and practice during the initial years of the Jerusalem community.

The *Teaching* predates the gospels and served as a transitional document during a time prior to the apostolic council. It was composed during an age when believers were called members of "the way" and it preserves a body of tradition that was verbally transmitted. The principal decrees are to love one's neighbor and to overcome sin, but it continues with guidance regarding baptism, fasting, prayer, Eucharist, liturgy, tithing, worship, and governance. Especially important is the role of itinerant apostles, prophets, and teachers who directed the community, together with local overseers and deacons. The final chapter contains an apocalyptic warning that summarizes apostolic signs that accompany the end of the age.

The manuscript measures seven and a half by six inches, and the scribe responsible for preserving the small, thick volume was named Leo(n). He wrote with a small, fluent, and distinctly characteristic style. Since the codex was discovered, other forms and fragments of the *Teaching* were found at various locations. It is listed in early Christian catalogs and was used as a catechism for Gentile converts to the faith. It is the most important text of its kind ever published, and it has prompted hundreds of modern editions, translations, articles, essays, and dissertations. No document has made as great an impact on studying the early church, and no work is more fundamental to understanding the origins of Christianity than the *Teaching*.

Brent S. Walters
Saint Joseph's Day
March 19, 2018

THE TEACHING OF THE TWELVE APOSTLES

TABLE OF CONTENTS

THE TEACHING OF THE TWELVE APOSTLES

Διδαχὴ κυρίου διὰ τῶν δώδεκα ἀποστόλων τοῖς ἔθνεσιν

They continued faithfully in the teaching of the apostles, in fellowship, in breaking of the loaf, and in prayers. Reverential awe overcame every soul, and many wonders and signs happened through the apostles. All the believers who gathered together shared all things in common, and they sold properties and possessions and then distributed to all those who had need. From day to day they remained with one mind in the Temple and broke bread from house to house, shared food in gladness and simplicity of heart, praised God, and had favor with all the people.[1]

The Teaching of the Twelve Apostles is an early Christian document that reflects the conditions of the Jesus movement as described in the first half of the Acts narrative prior to admitting Gentiles as full members of the church. It was not until the Jerusalem council that such integration became normative,[2] after the extensive efforts of Paul and his companions and the encouragement of James the Just, the brother of Jesus. However, the Teaching circulated prior to this conference, and since it retains some Pharisaic themes this may suggest the intent of its editor. Confirming its early date are: 1) the simplicity of style and language, 2) the identification of "the way," 3) the use of Hebraisms, 4) the early forms of baptism, prayer, and liturgy, 5) the implicit Christology, 6) the transitional character of the ministry, and 7) the local arrangements of church funds. Furthermore, the text is free from content associated with sectarian movements, is absent of any legendary setting, and is a compilation of verbally transmitted Jesus sayings prior to the publication of the canonical accounts.

The Teaching is divided into three main sections and was used as a catechism, that is, a body of instruction taught to those about to be initiated by means of baptism. For this reason, its content is neither innovative nor dogmatic; its readers were learning the basic tenets of the faith in order to receive admittance into the local community of believers as well as access to the agape meal and to the Eucharistic celebration. Its first portion is known as the two ways, and it is comprised of authentic instruction attributed to the apostles concerning how to love one's neighbor, overcome sin, function within the community, and participate in the church. Many of these themes provide a summary of oral tradition containing the ethical teachings of Jesus, portions of which were later preserved in the synoptic gospels.

---

[1] Acts 2:42-47. Notice that the phrase "teaching of the apostles" is used in this passage as if it represents an acknowledged body of tradition. The remaining reference indicates a spiritual gathering with a meal and public prayers. Those in need received assistance from others who distributed from their wealth, and they met daily in house churches and in the Temple.

[2] Acts 15. The apostolic council was the pivotal event in the Book of Acts, for those who attended discussed problematic issues that arose during this transition in early church history. The debate was over the full recognition of Gentiles into local communities associated with the Jesus movement without full compliance to the Jewish law. Some of the apostles, including Peter, and a few companions of Paul, met to address their integration. Three prohibitions were established: abstaining from blood, meat offered to idols, and sexual immorality. James, the brother of Jesus, penned and circulated the council's decision. Some did not feel the measures were restrictive enough, and many of them insisted that circumcision be obligatory; it is likely that those belonging to this sect became the Judaizers who taunted Paul throughout his ministry.

Application in the document is practical, for rather than citing commandments, the Teaching defines the sources of sin as well as a means for recovery, redemption, and restoration.

The second section includes advice regarding baptism, fasting, prayer, Eucharist, clergy, tithing, worship, and church administration. Especially important is its description of the early liturgical service in addition to the role of itinerant apostles, prophets, and teachers who governed the community, together with local overseers and deacons. The final chapter of the Teaching contains an apocalyptic warning that summarizes apostolic notions regarding signs that accompany the end of the age. This was an integral aspect of first-century theology, for the imminent return of Christ was understood as preceding the arrival of the kingdom of God. This document is roughly the size of an epistle and serves as a superb example of what early believers considered essential doctrine and practice during the initial years of the Jerusalem community; however, its place of origin and intended audience are difficult to ascertain. The manual shows no sign of Pauline or Johannine influence.

TOME FROM ANTIQUITY

Philotheos Bryennios was born at Constantinople in 1833, and as a youth he demonstrated academic prowess. He was educated at the theological institution at Chalki, where he returned after further training at the universities of Leipzig, Munich, and Berlin. He was selected professor in 1861, and six years later he relocated to become head of the Patriarchal School in Constantinople. Bryennios was appointed metropolitan of Serrae, Macedonia, in 1875, and was transferred to Nicomedia two years later. It was during this time that he found a remarkable manuscript in the section of Constantinople called Phanar; it would later be housed in the Jerusalem Monastery of the Holy Sepulcher. The folio was comprised of 120 pages of a small octavo codex that escaped the view of scholars who previously sought rare tomes and volumes for museums and royal collections. The text preserved some of the earliest Christian writings, including the epistles of Clement, Ignatius, Barnabas, as well as the Teaching.

The discovery was not immediately announced to the public, for the text of Clement was widely debated, since the manuscript that contained it was tattered and suffered several lacunae. In contrast, Bryennios's new discovery represented the finest to date, so in the introduction to his 1875 edition the metropolitan described its contents with greater detail. The text was written in a cursive font and was dated 1056, two years after the schism between the Eastern and Western churches;[3] it measured seven and a half by six inches. The

---

[3] The Great Schism refers to the official separation between the sees of Rome and Constantinople, after a long and bitter struggle. It occurred in 1054, at which time John the Faster proclaimed that he was universal bishop, an act that provoked an indignant response from Gregory I. Four principal differences separated the East from the West: 1) pope's claim of supremacy, 2) disputed jurisdiction in Sicily and southern Italy, 3) iconoclasm in the East, and 4) ritual and ceremonial differences in the liturgy, such as the arrangement of the service, language employed, vestments worn, use of incense, marriage of the clergy, unleavened bread in the West, wearing of beards in the East. The schism was far less about theology than about customs and practices, and it made a monumental mark on church history.

scribe's name was Leo(n),[4] and the small, thick, black volume was later named the Jerusalem Codex.[5] Since patristic scholars knew the documents contained in the manuscript, each belonging to the era immediately succeeding the apostles, they were assigned to the period after the fall of Jerusalem, roughly 70-140, except for the Teaching. That particular text was cited or listed in catalogs from the first four hundred years of the church, including those of Eusebius[6] and Athanasius,[7] and no other work of its kind survived antiquity.

Consequently, Western academics were particularly interested to learn more about the treatise, and a few prominent patristic scholars inquired of Bryennios the substance of the Teaching of the Twelve Apostles; a brief description was subsequently provided. After publishing his edition on Clement, the Greek prelate returned to the manuscript for a second evaluation of its contents and only then did he realize the monumental value of the codex. He immediately set out to write a volume exclusively dedicated to the Teaching, a text that remained relatively unknown until he published it in December 1883 entirely in scholastic Greek. Professors, historians and clerics around the world were persuaded that Bryennios's discovery represented an essential link missing in ecclesiastical history and that it contained information that would transform the modern view of early Christian thought and practice. Little did anyone suspect the impact that the brief text would make on the academic world, for over the next twelve months it was featured in at least one hundred books, articles, newspapers, and patrologies.

The full title of the document is "Teaching of the Twelve Apostles to the Gentiles," and even a cursory reading of its subject matter demonstrates that the manual comprises the earliest known catechism of the church.[8] The phrase "teaching of the apostles" is used in Acts 2:42 to represent a synopsis of what the initial members of the Jerusalem community considered essential doctrine and practice during the primitive years of the movement. Despite its title, this anthology of apostolic tradition does not assert that the twelve, or any one among them, actually composed its contents, only that their principles are summarized in its concise statements, since they no longer resided in the holy city. In fact, it appears to be based on oral instruction dating to the earliest age of the Jerusalem community, with some borrowed from synagogue instruction, at an important pivotal interim before Gentiles were admitted to the church. This reflects matters addressed in Acts 15, when the apostolic council convened to determine the conditional measures necessary for their participation in local Jewish congregations.

---

[4] The scribal note reads: "Finished in the month of June, upon the 11th (of the month), day 3d (of the week, i.e., Tuesday), Indiction 9, of the year 6564. By the hand of Leo(n), notary and sinner."

[5] The Jerusalem Codex, also called Hierosolymitanus and the Bryennios Manuscript is often designated simply "H" among scholars. "Jerusalem" refers to its housing in that city at the library belonging to the monastery of the Church of the Holy Sepulchre in the Christian quarter of the old city.

[6] Church History 3:25. Eusebius claimed that the Teaching was counted among the "rejected" writings, together with the Shepherd of Hermas, Apocalypse of Peter, and Epistle of Barnabas, and Apocalypse of John.

[7] Festal Letters, 39. The bishop of Alexandria, Athanasius, assigned the Teaching among those documents appointed for reading and instruction but were not included in the canon: Wisdom of Solomon, Wisdom of Sirach, Esther, Judith, Tobit, the Teaching of the Apostles, and the Shepherd of Hermas.

[8] The term "catechism" refers to an authorized collection of oral or written instructions that summarizes or explains essential doctrines for new converts, especially those related to the sacraments. These contents were usually recited, and often memorized, as described in the Teaching.

There is no indication that the compiler of this catechism used material other than that attributed to the apostles, for his task primarily involved the arrangement and sequence of its contents. The work contains no statement that contradicts Jesus or that is recorded in the Book of Acts; in fact, it shares a great deal in common with the Epistle of James and the Gospel of Matthew. Hence, a Jewish editor is expected, perhaps a moderate Pharisaic convert to the faith. Unlike later documents that comprise collections of sayings, the Teaching does not claim to come from the pen of the apostles or from one of their disciples. In several ways it parallels statements that are included in the canonical accounts and contains an early written form of the oral gospel. The editor organized his material in three sections; the first describes differences between the ways of life and death, the second pronounces moral instruction and church practice as well as sacred rituals and standard behavior. The third recapitulates apocalyptic thought regarding the *parousia*,[9] the imminent return of Christ.

A great deal of the document's first portion is echoed in earlier Jewish texts and later Christian works, and this includes the Epistle of Barnabas[10] and the Shepherd of Hermas,[11] both of which include a version of the two ways section. While the Teaching predates both of these prominent works, its editor seems to have borrowed from a related Jewish catechism for Gentiles. Its purpose was to provide essential principles prior to baptism, since it was a catechism; in fact, it was taught, applied, and recited to guarantee that this act of initiation was fully understood, as well as the rules that governed the community that they were about to represent. However, no specific New Testament gospel or epistle is cited; instead, significant statements from Jesus are condensed with many parallels later published in the Sermon on the Mount and in other prominent collections of sayings. Some scholars suggest that at its core is a well-circulated compilation like "Q"[12] that gained authority prior to the written gospels and was integrated into Matthew and Luke, but such a source seems to postdate the Teaching.

---

[9] The *parousia* is associated with the second advent of Christ. The word connotes "presence," in the sense of the bodily arrival of a person, and was used for the official visit of high-ranking people. From this notion came the simple understanding of "arrival" or "advent." A *parousia* was not limited to the future but was experienced in the present as a reality. When the term was used more technically it assumed a more cultic meaning, like the arrival of a hidden divinity who would make its presence felt through revelation. This sense of the term was carried over into the Septuagint and was employed in apocalyptic circles, where it came to refer to the coming of Messiah.

[10] Barnabas 18-21. There is a parallel version of the two ways recorded in the Epistle of Barnabas. It appears to be an expansion of the standard text and begins, "There are two ways of teaching and power, one of light and one of darkness, and there is a great difference between the two ways. Over the one are set light-bearing angels of God, but over the other are angels of Satan, and the one is Lord from eternity to eternity, while the other is ruler of the present time of iniquity. The way of light is this: if any man desire to journey to the appointed place, he should be zealous in his works."

[11] Hermas, Mandates 6:1.1. The Shepherd of Hermas similarly contains a form of the two ways document applying different terminology, "I now wish, he said, to explain also their qualities so that you may understand what is the quality of each and its operation, for their function is of two kinds. They relate, then to the righteous and to the unrighteous. You should therefore believe the righteous, but do not believe the unrighteous. That which is righteous has a straight path, while that which is unrighteous a crook path. However, you should walk in the straight path and leave the crooked path alone."

[12] "Q" (from the German *Quelle* meaning "source") is the symbol used to designate a non-Marcan source common both to Matthew and Luke. If "Q" was a written text, then it must have belonged to an authoritative collection of isolated and detached sayings with some discourse material. It seems to have circulated by the year 50, and may represent the earliest source of gospel instruction to survive antiquity.

While the content of this document seems apostolic in character, it apparently fell out of use after the acceptance of Gentiles, the spread of Pauline theology, and the rise of diverse schools of thought. Perhaps for these reasons the two ways section was detached and was independently assimilated into later works. The publication of more complete collections of oral tradition also contributed, as did the Jerusalem council and the gathering of canonical works after the close of the apostolic age. Numerous factors contributed to a decrease of the Teaching's use, therefore, not the least of which was the circulation of Mark's gospel, for that narrative provided the explanation for its instruction. Furthermore, as time passed, the dynamic between Jews and Gentiles dramatically changed, especially after the center of church authority relocated at Pella in the Decapolis.[13] There was no longer a need for subtle references to the Pharisees or Sadducees or to adapted customs borrowed from the synagogue after the year 70.

The catechism was not forgotten but integrated, whether fully or in part, into later forms until it was ultimately integrated into comprehensive church orders over the ensuing four centuries. It seems apparent that Justin possessed a copy of the work or was instructed from one similar to the Teaching, since the outline of his apology was based on such a document; furthermore, other patristic writers cited from the manual with authority. However, it seems as though the treatise did not make much of an impact in the West, except in its Latin form, and that may explain its disappearance in Christian literature by the rise of Constantine. The Teaching was transitional and was composed prior to the events described in Acts 15; as a result, it must have circulated before the year 50. While not reading like a crisis document, it bears the marks of a foundational text, the chief intent of which was to deal with a sudden influx of Gentile converts into primarily Jewish communities.

This may imply that its editor was familiar with oral and written tradition and was trained in the Pharisaic school of thought. In that respect, the catechism shares a great deal in common with *Pirkei Avot*,[14] a compilation of ethical and practical precepts associated with various Jewish sages from Simon the Just (200 BCE) to Judah ha-Nasi (200 CE). During these four centuries, the oral law ascribed to such legal scholars was collated and organized prior to its publication in written form. This process ultimately resulted in the Mishnah,[15] the definitive accumulation of prominent proverbs, mandates, aphorisms, and both legal prescripts

---

[13] Pella (modern Tabaqat Fahil) was a member of the Decapolis, "ten cities," across and east of the Jordan River. It is an extremely ancient site that dates prior to Canaanite occupation before the days of Abraham, but in the first century it thrived with a rich Hellenistic culture. The city was destroyed before the Israelite conquest, and Greek colonists rebuilt it after the reign of Alexander the Great. Since these settlers were Macedonians, its name changed from Pahel to Pella, the famous capital of Macedonia and the birthplace of Alexander. Warned through a prophecy about the destruction of Jerusalem, the Christian community left the holy city for Pella in 66, the year the first Jewish War with Rome began (Eusebius, History 3:5).

[14] Pirkei Avot is the most cited and reprinted Talmudic work; it belongs to the Mishnah and contains five chapters separated into four sections. Its purpose was to establish a divine origin for the Torah, in both its oral and written forms, to show continuity in its transmission, and to define the ethical standards that governed all Jewish conduct, especially that with regard to the study, administration, and fulfillment of the law. The sayings are arranged in chronological order and were probably compiled during the life of Judah ha-Nasi, since his son is the last sage cited. Its content reflects the various convictions that shaped the Pharisaic schools.

[15] The Mishnah contains a codified collection of oral laws that the Pharisees maintained, arranged, redacted, and revised around the year 210 at the hand of Judah ha-Nasi. It prominently features the sayings of Hillel and Shammai as well as other contemporary sages and rabbis. The Mishnah is divided into six parts

and interpretations. Similarly, the Teaching is a collection of sayings attributed to the apostles or to their associates during the earliest age of the church, and it too was based on verbal instruction and was only later distributed as a compilation of precepts and practices. Both documents summarize the essence of moral behavior that each expects of its adherents and proselytes. However, in contrast, the catechism reflects no more than two decades of oral tradition attributed to the twelve whom Jesus selected.

Due to its inclusion in later church orders, the original form of the Teaching was expanded, and this may explain why it was not explicitly cited in later Alexandrian or Antiochene theological literature. Nonetheless, Clement of Alexandria[16] was familiar with the Teaching and cited from it near the close of the second century, together with 1 Clement, Epistle of Barnabas, Gospel according to the Hebrews, Shepherd of Hermas, Apocalypse of Peter, and other widely-circulated documents. A century and a half later, Athanasius catalogued the catechism among writings that were read with authority but were not regarded as scripture, for he developed what ultimately became the first official Christian canon. In essence, he retained its value and usefulness, especially among those learning the rudimentary elements of the faith. In his thirty-ninth festal letter, Athanasius identified twenty-seven books that comprised the New Testament, with seven beneficial and popular texts not included but encouraged to be read, among them was the Teaching.

This establishes, therefore, that the catechism was still in use as late as 367, when Athanasius issued his catalog of inspired documents; hence, it may have been read as scripture in some significant centers of the church. In Caesarea, for example, Eusebius accepted the Teaching as non-canonical but widely read, together with the Shepherd of Hermas, Apocalypse of Peter, Epistle of Barnabas, and Apocalypse of John. It seems evident that each of these documents was housed in Pamphilus's library,[17] thus, the historian had continued access to them. By this late date, it appears that the catechism was acknowledged as a summary of basic tenets of the faith and was useful as a source of instruction. All the same, it gradually fell into disuse, since much larger works replaced its simplicity with detailed regulations that governed local communities and theological principles that reflected a later

---

with sixty-three treatises covering laws dealing with agricultural produce, feasts, women, property rights, holy things in the Temple, and the purity laws. Therefore, by evaluating its contents some of the religious environment at the time of Jesus may be recovered, especially that which influenced Paul the apostle, since he was educated as a Pharisee in the school of Hillel.

[16] Clement of Alexandria was probably born at Athens of non-Christian parents around the middle of the second century and died between 211 and 216. His extensive use of Greek literature affirms the excellence of his education, for which he traveled throughout Greece, Italy, Palestine, and Egypt. Clement followed Pantaenus as director of the catechetical school of Alexandria, where, as a distinguished teacher he addressed his literary treatises to the highly educated, while striving to blend Christianity and Greek culture. He was quite unique in this approach.

[17] Pamphilus was born into a wealthy, noble family in Phoenicia and became a presbyter of Caesarea; he was the most preeminent Christian scholar of his day. His generosity supplied poor scholars the texts necessary for learning, for he devoted his life to procuring ancient documents with which he established a famous library that housed 30,000 volumes. He also founded a theological school in which his students reproduced manuscripts for distribution. Pamphilus oversaw the production of corrected copies of scripture and was central to the preservation of the biblical text as well as patristic literature. He died a martyr in the third year of the Diocletian persecution (306). His influence cannot be exaggerated, for he provided the basis for Eusebius's monumental church history, the preservation of Origen's literary contributions, and the origin of textual criticism.

age of the church. The content in the Teaching restricts its place of origin to a region where Paul's ministry did not initially reach, since it contains none of his technical terminology or cites from any of his epistles.

The Teaching, therefore, appears to represent a branch of early Jewish Christianity, one possibly residing in Galilee or Judea or one that those communities founded. However, this does not suggest that its editors were hostile to the apostolic school of thought, nor for that matter Pharisaic ethical precepts. Consequently, it was not written in response to the evangelical efforts of some sectarian branch of the church, like the Ebionites, or of any of the sundry docetic communities.[18] Its sources were apostolic, at least in topic and content, and of the four canonical accounts, the Teaching is closest to Matthew, based on its words, phrases, and motifs, although the compiler did not directly borrow from any extant written form of the gospel. This may suggest a northern region where believers in the Diaspora were known to flourish. It makes little sense to conclude that the document was composed as late as the resettlement of the Jerusalem community at Pella in 66, for by that time the Gentiles were fully integrated into church customs, beliefs, and governance.

It seems that the catechism enjoyed circulation beyond its place of origin, and this implies that it either derived from a well-established center of the faith or was used for a brief period at a critical juncture when various schools of thought challenged the integrity of the gospel message. Hence, the Teaching is one of the most illusive documents of the first century and may be assigned to the initial stage of Gentile conversion, one quite independent of Pauline influence and authority. While it is possible that the document was modeled after a Jewish manual of instruction for proselytes, no work of this kind or era has survived. If this were the case, then such a work was severely redacted in order to accommodate the needs of early Gentile believers, for it is critical of Pharisaic hypocrisy, formed a body of instruction, and permitted proselyte admission. Regarding its composition, there are several reasons to assign the Teaching to an early date, not the least of which is its lack of references to the life of Jesus or of his apostles.

Believers are identified as members of "the way," a phrase Saul of Tarsus used during his tirade against the Jerusalem faithful,[19] rather than "Christian,"[20] a term not yet embraced in that community. The catechism opens with the notion of choosing between two paths,

---

[18] The Ebionites were a sect around the destruction of Jerusalem that it did not come to prominence until after the Bar Kokhba revolt (132-136). Judaizers who strongly opposed Paul originated this schematic movement, and while most patristic writers identified their founder as Ebion, who lived in Pella after the church left Jerusalem, this is likely a product of legend. They insisted on the complete observance of Jewish law were intensely docetic (denied the physical essence of Christ), and were responsible for the Clementine literature. Their gospel was widely circulated throughout Syria and remained in use until the time of Jerome, who wrote extensively about it.

[19] Acts 9:2 and 19:23. Saul requested authoritative letters in order to access the synagogues of Damascus. His intent was to locate any who "belong to the way, men or women," so that he might bring them to Jerusalem in chains. Later in the narrative is the phrase, "about that time there arose a controversy concerning 'the way.'" This suggests a movement rather than a theological system.

[20] The term *Christian* implies "of the party of Christ," but it is used only three times in the New Testament (Acts 11:26, 26:28, and 1 Peter 4:16). This is because it was not a preferred name; believers instead were known as members of "the way." The term *Christian* originated at Antioch in the year 42, and it probably bore a negative connotation as if to distinguish this group from other sects among the Jews. By the beginning of the second century, however, the title was generally adopted.

for one leads to life and the other to death. This is perhaps the most recurring concept throughout Jewish scripture from the garden choice in Eden to prophetic warnings of infidelity. Its form of the gospel is oral rather than written, and it is not attributed to any specific author. The apostles are still principal leaders of the church, albeit in a secondary sense as Paul later appointed to office. Prophets exhort and serve the community while defining the movement and maintaining a leading role in the daily lives of believers. The document is behaviorally based but is not dogmatic, and it shows signs of primitive liturgy, prayer, and matters regarding church funds and administration. Other indicators of its early date are demonstrated in its multiple modes of baptism, its views regarding prayer, fasting, and alms, and its nascent apocalyptic worldview.

The full title of the document is the "Teaching of the Twelve Apostles to the Gentiles," but most scholars identify it with the Greek term *Didache*. It appears that the editor offered a temporary solution to the increase of non-Jewish converts in a region outside the Jerusalem community; however, after their admission, such a designation was no longer necessary. The term "Gentile" was derived from *ethnos*, connoting "custom" or "habit"; in essence, it classified proselytes into categories based on factors such as indigenous language, national origin, and cultural conventions that united and distinguished one nation from another. It was commonly used of a majority people in a pejorative sense, and in many ways it was equivalent to the label "foreigner." The Jews employed the term in reference to Gentiles as well as to those who did not maintain the same religious customs or beliefs or belong to the same genealogical lineage. In this sense, it connoted "nations," that most scribes and sages in antiquity considered to be seventy, the same number of disciples Jesus initially commissioned.

Such a designation suggests that some converts were associated with provinces or territories outside the traditional borders of Israel. As a result, the Teaching was particularly compiled for Gentile believers during a time when the church was primarily comprised of Jews dwelling in the homeland of the apostles. Such discrimination gradually faded, however, once they were viewed as members without distinction, for by that time there was less a need for such a catechism. Certainly its sections on the Eucharist and agape meal required integration of Jews and Gentiles as part of the same community, for they partook from the same table. Therefore, if the Book of Acts is used as the historical standard, the Teaching was composed after the twelve left the Jerusalem for the mission field and yet before the Jerusalem council, hence, between the years 42 and 50. This implies that it predates every work included in the New Testament, with the likely exception of the Epistle of James,[21] a related document that the brother of Jesus penned.

---

[21] James the Just was the eldest of Jesus' brothers named in the gospels (Matthew 13:54-56) as well as the epistles of Paul (1 Corinthians 9:5 and Galatians 1:18-19). He became leader of the Jerusalem community after the apostles set out for the mission field. Paul considered him a "pillar" of the church, and he presided over the apostolic council in the year 50, at which time the Gentiles were admitted into the church with few restrictions. Established church tradition describes James as a man of both philosophy and religion; he was righteous from birth, for he maintained a nazarite vow and worshipped in the Temple. His epistle was the earliest of those later incorporated into the New Testament, and his story was preserved at length in the writings of Hegesippus during the mid-second century, the first historian of the church, upon whom Eusebius was indebted (History 2:1).

As the earliest surviving Christian document, this letter shares a lot in common with the Teaching, for its recipients are addressed as "the twelve tribes in the Diaspora."[22] However, the relationship between these two works is more than audience, for both emphasize a similar overall theme and employ terminology too unguarded to date from a later age. In fact, they seem to derive from the same school of thought, one to which the Gospel of Matthew also belongs, although from a few decades later. Consequently, the compiler of the Teaching is possibly an unknown disciple of Jesus from a moderate Pharisaic school and perhaps a scribe, as the organization and style of the work suggest. If this were the case, then the objective of the editor was to summarize the gospel message for the newly converted, and it is unlikely that he intended to distinguish Jewish from Gentile readers since similar material was later preserved in the gospels. This might account for the two titles attached to the text, for only one mentions non-Jewish catechumens.

Pliny the Younger was a severe critic of the church during the reign of Trajan, to whom he composed an epistle between 110 and 112. It belongs to his tenth book dealing with issues that arose in the provinces of Bithynia and Pontus and contains the earliest Roman account of Christian behavior and provides the rationale for persecution. He admits not participating in their trials and therefore asks the emperor how to proceed against them. He affirmed that believers gathered on a specific day early in the morning, sung a hymn to Christ as to a god, and were bound to moral oaths. Later in the day they returned to eat an innocent meal; this apparently was the agape feast. Trajan responded that Christians should not be sought unless brought up on charges through official legal proceedings. All unverifiable accusations were to be ignored and any believer could recant his faith publicly and escape punishment. Pliny's details were based on secondhand, anonymous informants or were extracted by means of torture; nonetheless, it serves as the earliest Roman description of the faith.

> It is customary, my lord, to refer to you cases about which I am in doubt, for who can better offer guidance during my hesitation or clarify when I am ignorant? I have never participated in any legal trial against the Christians; therefore, I do not know the routine penalties inflicted on them, the limits to impose, or even how to investigate an inquiry. I have vacillated for some time considering whether any distinctions should be drawn concerning the ages of those accused or whether I should punish the weak as severely as the strong or whether the man who has been a Christian gains anything by denouncing or whether the man

---

[22] The meaning of *Diaspora* is "scattering" or "sowing of seeds," and it refers to Jews forced to live outside their traditional homeland, such as those residing in Syria, Anatolia, Babylonia, and Egypt, each of which had an estimated population of no fewer than a million Jews. The concept began during the Babylonian captivity in 597 BCE, and it continued well after the defeat of two Jewish revolts against Rome, both of which likewise contributed to Jews scattered beyond the borders of Judea. Two centuries before the destruction of that region, Jews dwelt throughout the cities of the Mediterranean world. Precise numbers cannot be confirmed; however, after Palestine and Babylonia, the largest congregation of Hellenistic Jews was in Syria, particularly at Antioch, and then at Damascus. Philo provides the number of Jewish inhabitants in Egypt as 1,000,000, roughly one-eighth of the population that occupied two of the five quarters of the city. This ultimately made Alexandria the most influential Jewish center.

who was once a Christian benefits from recanting or whether I should punish the name "Christian" even though otherwise the man is innocent of crime except those generally associated with the name....

Their sole guilt or error was the custom of meeting on a fixed day before dawn and singing a hymn to Christ as though he were a god. They publicly take an oath not to commit any crime, and they vow to abstain from fraud, theft, adultery, perjury, and to render trust money deposited with them when called upon to deliver it. When the ceremony is over they customarily depart in order to assemble again and to partake of food; however, it is ordinary and harmless food. They affirmed that even this ceased after my edict forbidding secret associations in accordance with your directive....

I therefore postponed the investigation and immediately consulted you, for the matter seemed to warrant your prompt consideration, especially due to the number of people involved.... Many people of various ages and of both genders are put in danger, for the contagion of this superstition has spread not only to cities but also to villages and farms.[23]

TWO WAYS DOCUMENT

The first section of the Teaching comprises a system of instruction designed to affirm the fundamentals of the faith. While it is preoccupied with ethical, didactical, and practical content regarding lifestyle and responsibility to the community, the second portion contains directives that identify customs, govern offices, and distinguish practices with emphasis on social structure and church administration. The final section preserves early Christian thought regarding the return of Jesus and the end of the world and provides an apocalyptic warning of its imminence. The entire document serves as the earliest witness to church tradition prior to the prominence of Paul and his unique approach to matters relating to the integration of males and females, Jews and Greeks, rich and poor.[24] While scholars do not agree on date or circulation of the Teaching, the nascent state of the community it describes reflects the opening chapters of Acts. It certainly is not as late as the gospels or epistles preserved in the New Testament.

The catechism makes mention of customs among the Jews that were practiced prior to the fall of Jerusalem, especially those of the Pharisees, who apparently were still walking the streets of the holy city and persecuting believers. It certainly dates earlier than the year 66 when the church in that city migrated to Pella in the Decapolis or relocated to Judea, Anatolia, Alexandria, or Rome. Furthermore, by that late date there was little need for a

---

[23] Pliny the Younger, Letters 10.96-97. This citation was edited for the purpose of brevity. No significant content regarding the early church or believers in general was deliberately redacted.

[24] Galatians 3:28. Paul emphatically asserted that whether the believer is a Jew or a Greek, whether a slave or a freedman, whether a male or a female, all are one in Christ Jesus, for the communities he established did not make such distinctions. This sort of rhetoric is what fostered groups such as the Judaizers to oppose the apostle in most regions he preached. At one point, they were determined either to kill Paul or have him arrested in Jerusalem due to his interpretation of the law.

document outlining instruction for Gentile converts, since it is probable that they comprised the majority in most communities. In fact, it seems unlikely that the Teaching was composed after the apostolic council, because the decree that James circulated dealt with the issues that prevented full membership. Moreover, the details of this edict are not precisely replicated in the catechism as if its composition predates Luke's chronicle. The same is true of the Pauline corpus, since the Jerusalem edict was applied in his communities as part of a theological directive.

Modern scholars have thoroughly examined its text, and most have integrated the work into their editions of church history, since its discovery one hundred and forty years ago. In this respect, it is perceived as a transitional treatise that was circulated to insure a place for all believers in the local community. It has been translated dozens of times into English and into every modern language, while its Greek text has been fully analyzed and textual critics have collated all related manuscripts, fragments, and versions. Furthermore, experts have extracted it from later church orders and have compared it to documents from those eras, and yet the Teaching remains elusive to most of the public. Hundreds of editions, monographs, articles, essays, and dissertations are published on this brief document, more than for any other early Christian work apart from the New Testament, and yet its content is seldom mentioned from pulpits, podiums, or platforms.

The concept of two ways was not foreign to the ancient religious world, for the Greeks were fond of the metaphor and frequently employed it. In fact, from the dawn of Western civilization the notion was popular in literature beginning with Hesiod. He described the road to vice as smooth, but to reach virtue a long, steep path required the sweat of our brows. He taught that while it was rough at first, once an individual reached its top virtue was easy to attain.[25] Similarly, the pre-Socratics understood life as filled with decisions, either good and bad. The moral is found after traveling a long and treacherous path that initially is rife with struggle but eases as the journey reaches its pinnacle. The immoral is observed in all aspects of daily existence and is common to all people of every nation; it is a natural response to life, one that the populace chooses without contemplation or concern. Its journey begins effortlessly and bears few burdens, but in the end it proves to be worthless.

Between moral and immoral the gods placed the labor and conduct of life, for the struggle not only involves decisions but also requires conflicts encountered from those walking on the opposite path. The legend of Heracles exemplifies this process,[26] for this deity noticed early in life that virtue and vice appear in different personas. The former is fair, pure, and sober; the latter is plump, weak, and trite. While morality is radiant white, immorality casts

---

[25] Works and Days 287-292. Hesiod was an early Greek writer who was active around 700 BCE; he was a contemporary of Homer and was among the earliest written poets of Western antiquity. Hesiod is especially remembered for preserving religious customs; in fact, he became the main source for Greek mythology. He wrote extensively on several fields of interest, and numerous legends circulated about him. His two most renowned works are Theogony, that describes the myths, and Works and Days, that depicts peasant life, both of which are vital to understanding the origin of Hellenistic culture.

[26] Heracles was born at Alcaeus, the son of Zeus and Alcmene, and assumed a divine role in Greek mythology. He was regarded as the greatest of the heroes. In Rome and most of the Western world he is known as Hercules; however, the Greek version of his life remained essentially unchanged, except for scattered details. The most famous story regarding him is "The Twelve Labors of Heracles."

a deceptive shadow. The task of every person is to decide between these two ways, although only evil seems to make an attempt to entice an individual. In the end, good is obtained in its own quietness, while evil parades with reckless abandon. Such is the struggle between the paths of life and death, and this is experienced in the everyday choices of humans. While this Greek version of the metaphor was popular beyond the reach of its initial influence, the Hellenistic version maintained in the church is preserved in the Teaching.

The same concept is described in prophetic literature by means of a two ways metaphor with one choice representing life and the other death. It was a favorite among the Jewish sages and was expressed in the visions of Jeremiah, "I set before you the way of life and the way of death."[27] This prophet was indebted to the traditions of Moses as preserved in Deuteronomy, "I have set before you this day life and good, death and evil."[28] This notion developed during the prophetic age when the Israelites were commanded to choose between the path of righteousness or that of wickedness. Isaiah echoed the allegory, "This is the way, so walk in it whenever you turn to the right or turn to the left."[29] While these two ways were explained among the prophets, they were established in Eden, for a tree stood in the midst of the garden possessing the knowledge of good and of evil, both of which were products of choice. The command was to remain on the path that averted destruction, hence, a decision couched in consequence.

While unwavering obedience results in immortality, waywardness eventually leads to ruin. The garden choice, therefore, depicts specific realms of knowledge, and both paths involve conscious discernment that develop with experience. In essence, sin is about human choice rather than human nature, for life and death are journeys down well-trodden paths that require acknowledgment of their destinations. As a result, the Creator would not invalidate the Eden choice, for it represents a lifelong pursuit of virtue and proper decisions, neither of which the couple chose. Instead, they visited the tree from which they were forbidden to partake, and out of this notion gradually developed the concept of sin. It was not the serpent in garden that caused their fall but the tree where the cunning beast manifested. Hence, to approach the tree was to tread a path that veered from the way of life, the consequence of which was the loss of immortality.

Wisdom literature is replete with the two ways metaphor, for the path of the Lord is comprised of proper choices, as stated in the first Psalm, "The Lord knows the way of the righteous, but the way of the wicked will perish." The proverbial form of this concept also requires human decision, "There is a way that seems right to a man, but its end is the way

---

[27] Jeremiah 21:8. The Lord is described as establishing only two choices, life or death. This indicates that sin was not viewed as the product of nature, during the time of the prophets, but of choice, since the twofold path was offered but required a singular response. This provides insight into the prophet's perspective about potential peace for the Israelites, provided they choose the proper path.

[28] Deuteronomy 30:15. Moses instructed the Israelites that life and good represent one path and death and evil another. Keeping the Lord's commandments, statutes, and ordinances is called "walking in his ways." However, if the Israelites turn their hearts and worship other gods they will perish. "I have set before you life and death, blessing and curse; therefore, choose life" (30:15-19).

[29] Isaiah 30:21. The prophet depicts a designated path that leads to different destinations. The choice is whether the individual taking the journey turns to the right or to the left. In this respect it is choice between two paths, one of life and the other of death. Since the theme of the first section is judgment about to fall on sinful Israelites, the prophet delivers oracles on judgment and redemption.

to death";[30] similarly, "In the path of righteousness is life, while the path of error leads to death."[31] Contemporary wisdom tradition maintained the same sentiment, "Before each man are life and death and whichever he chooses will be given to him."[32] Two texts discovered at Qumran, and preserved in the Dead Sea Scrolls,[33] contain references to this allegory; while one involves the way of light, the other describes the way of darkness.[34] It is not surprising, therefore, that the gospel message was conceived amidst this cultural understanding of human choice between two destinations, for this was proclaimed in the declaration of John the Baptist. His role in the narrative was directly related to the purpose of Messiah, for he was described as a voice crying in the desert, "Prepare the way of the Lord; make his paths straight."[35]

This perspective is maintained, even explained, in the saying of Jesus, "Enter through the narrow gate, because wide is the gate and broad is the way leading to destruction and there are many entering through it; however, straight is the gate and narrower still is the way leading to life and few there are who find it."[36] In essence, every individual chooses between two paths, and gates identify the destination of each traveler. If the journey's road requires difficult moral decisions and personal struggles successfully executed, it leads to life. In contrast, if no inward conflicts are resolved and the sojourner bears no concern for others, his destination is death. This was the principal message that the emerging community instructed, based on the sayings of the apostles and summarized in the opening section of the Teaching. At its core the early gospel message concerned two choices; one embracing immortality, the other denouncing it. This is why its first section contains instruction on the way of life that includes the basic tenets of the faith.

---

[30] Proverbs 14:12. It is not surprising that the psalms and proverbs echo the need to distinguish righteous from wicked behavior, since both require human decision.

[31] Proverbs 12:28. Notice that righteousness is a human decision and that death is the result of a path that extends to the grave.

[32] Sirach 15:17. The content in Sirach is generally attributed to Simeon, the son of Yeshua, the son of Eleazar, the son of Sira (Ben Sira). The book is comprised of wisdom literature and is assigned to 180-175 BCE. Ben Sira belonged to a class of sages that was celebrated alongside the priests and prophets of his age. What makes this document unique is that rather than preserve various sages, it contains the contribution of a single writer in Jerusalem. Sirach was frequently cited in Jewish and Christian literature and was spoken on the streets as proverbial wisdom.

[33] The Dead Sea Scrolls is an ancient collection of manuscripts initially discovered in 1947 in one of the caves in the cliffs of the west coast of the Dead Sea, roughly eight and a half miles south of Jericho. It contains an assortment of biblical, apocryphal, sectarian, and apocalyptic writings as part of the Judean Desert Documents. Most scrolls were written in Hebrew and represent diverse schools of Jewish thought, some espousing the views of certain sects such as the Essenes. Nine hundred eighty-one different fragments and texts were found in eleven different caves over a ten-year period. Scholars assign most of them to the last three centuries BCE to the first century CE.

[34] 1QS 3:18-4:26. The Community Rule (1QS) is one of the first of seven scrolls discovered at Qumran; it is a sectarian treatise from a separatist faction. The text contains rules and regulations for their particular community. Since multiple copies were found in the caves, it must have been central to their cause and must have governed those dwelling in the region.

[35] Mark 1:3. The path is attributed to the Lord, for the faithful are to prepare his way and to make his paths straight. It is related also to John the Baptist, for he was preaching a baptism of repentance for the forgiveness of sins. In essence, he was preparing a righteous community.

[36] Matthew 7:13-14. This is one of several parallels between the Teaching and Matthew; in fact, the Sermon on the Mount is a series of sayings like those attributed to the twelve in the catechism. This implies that they belong to that or a similar community, perhaps one dwelling in the same region.

This theme inspired early patristic writers to expound the choice with more detail. Ignatius of Antioch was among the first to attempt it; he was martyred at the beginning of the second century, "The choice is between two things, death and life, and each goes to his own destination; similarly, there are two coinages, one of God and the other of the world, and each has its own stamp impressed on it."[37] In this sense, the two ways represent decision, for while immortality was provided by means of redemption, the recipient must actively engage in its benefits. Consequently, the proper path is a lifestyle, not a philosophy, and for this reason the original title given to the Jerusalem movement was "the way." Shortly after the gospel message was introduced to the Gentiles, a catechism was compiled to instruct these new converts about the virtues and values of choosing the course leading to life. This is precisely what is preserved in the Teaching of the Twelve Apostles, for it opens with the phrase, "There are two ways, one of life and the other of death, and there is a great difference between these two ways."

LOVE YOUR NEIGHBOR

The Epistle to Diognetus is an anonymous treatise that a brilliant and articulate apologist composed on behalf of believers worldwide. The author was a renowned leader or founder of the church, considering the authority he exhibits, who defended the gospel message before emperors, senators, governors, or magistrates. A sixth century Syriac manuscript asserts that Ambrosius composed the work; he was "a principal man of Greece who became a Christian," but this cannot be established with certainty. The recipient likewise remains unknown, despite attempts to make him the tutor of Marcus Aurelius. The apologist establishes the superiority of the faith over Hellenistic and Jewish religious traditions with a series of well-crafted inquiries and arguments. His treatment of Christian identity under Roman rule is particularly enduring. Based on content and language, the "epistle" may be assigned to the sub-apostolic age, roughly 110-125. Due to a few lacunae, portions of the text are uncertain, and the document ends without a formal conclusion.

The distinction between Christians and the rest of humanity is neither in location, speech, or customs, for they do not inhabit cities of their own, nor do they use some unique dialect or practice an extraordinary kind of life. They do not possess any innovation that the intelligence or study of ingenious men has discovered, nor are they masters of any human doctrine as are other men. However, while they dwell in Greek and barbarian cities, as each has obtained his lot, and follow the local customs with regard to attire and diet and the rest of life, they demonstrate the wonderful and admittedly unexpected constitution of their

---

[37] Ignatius, Magnesians 5. Ignatius of Antioch was a prominent church leader from the close of the first century. His most lasting contribution was a set of letters penned on the way to his Roman execution. These epistles were so influential that three recensions circulated by the end of the fourth century. The author defended the churches of Anatolia (Smyrna, Ephesus, Magnesia, Tralles, and Philadelphia) as well as Rome against the increasing threat of heresy, especially that the Docetists introduced as well as the various Judaizing sects that infiltrated the church. His main theme was unity within church leadership.

own citizenship. They live in their own countries, but only as sojourners; they share all things as citizens and they endure all hardships as strangers. Every foreign country is a fatherland to them, and every fatherland is foreign.

They marry like all other men and they bear children and yet they do not expose their progeny. They share meals in common and yet not the bed. They exist in the flesh and yet they do not live after the flesh. They pass time upon the earth and yet their citizenship is in heaven. They obey the established laws and yet they surpass the laws in their own lives. They love all men and yet all men persecute them. They are unknown and yet they are condemned. They are put to death and yet they gain life. They are poor and yet make many rich. They lack all things and yet have all things in abundance. They are verbally dishonored and yet are glorified in their disgrace. They are denigrated and yet are vindicated. They are reviled and yet they bless. They are insulted and yet show respect.

When they act admirably they are punished as wicked, and when punished they rejoice as if by this means they receive life. The Jews wage war against them as foreigners and the Greeks persecute them, and yet those who hate them cannot state the reason for their hostility.[38]

The Teaching shares a great deal in common with the Epistle to Diognetus, especially its corollary directives that include a wide range of applications, each of which strengthens the community while promoting love of one's neighbor. The Teaching summarizes the essence of Jewish law by using a definition that Jesus instructed his disciples about the responsibility of believers toward one another. As the premier characteristic of the church, it was introduced as the paramount principle of the catechism and classified under the heading "the way of life," since believers were to love God who made them and their neighbors to the same degree as their own lives. This confirms the Lord's directive to the covenant people,[39] and hence it became a recurring theme throughout scripture. During the generation after the Temple's destruction, Akiva identified it as the fundamental principle of the Torah.[40] His contemporaries understood it as the initial impulse of creation, and many first-century sages, including Hillel and Shammai, interpreted the passage as applying to all humanity.

Loving one's neighbor was generally perceived as a genuine concern for the welfare of others as well as the advance of peace among all nations. The caveat, of course, is expressed

---

[38] Diognetus 5-6. The epistle was unknown until Henricus Stephanus published it in 1592, after he found it in a thirteenth-century manuscript. It remained the sole witness to the text but was lost in a fire. Hence, all that survived were transcripts copied from that codex. The probable place of composition is Athens, like the Apology of Aristides, for both works maintain a simple but profound understanding of the faith and both date from same period, perhaps around 124.

[39] Leviticus 19:18. The verse reads, "You shall not take vengeance or bear any grudge against the sons of your own people, but you shall love your neighbor as yourself: I am the LORD."

[40] Akiva Ben Joseph (c. 50-135) was one of the foremost scholars of his day. He was born in Judea of humble parentage, but his life was one of the most spectacular in rabbinic history. He was trained at the great academy at Lydda under the tutelage of the finest teachers of the day. He was a patriot and a martyr who exercised decisive influence over the development of the halakhah. Akiva is also credited with systematizing the Midrash halakhot and aggadot. He took a deep interest in the plight of the poor and made numerous journeys to collect funds on their behalf.

in the phrase, "as one's self," and for this Hillel[a] provided a useful explanation in a set of questions, "If I am not for me, who will be for me, and if I am only for me, what am I?" These sorts of inquiries resulted in a moral conundrum among the sages, for what should transpire if two men are in the desert and there is only enough water for one of them. Ben Petura replied, "Let the two of them drink, though both will die," while Akiva asserted that one life must take precedence over another, for he could not agree that both men should die. Such debate ultimately led to the perspective that the righteous must love all neighbors to the extent of self-sacrificing, for the true meaning of the precept is loving one's neighbor even more than one's own life. Jesus likewise summarized the statement regarding loving God and one's neighbor, and he did so in a reply, "Teacher, which is the greatest commandment in the law?"[b]

Consequently, there is little confusion why this statement opens the catechism, for love towards God with all one's heart, soul, and mind is the primary decree. The second is similar to it, since loving a neighbor in the same manner as one's own soul demonstrates the integrity of the dictum. These two directives not only govern proper behavior but also fulfill the law and the prophets, since that was to be the distinguishing quality of the covenant people. A parallel series of inquiries are implied throughout the two ways section, for how can a believer claim a love for the Lord and yet treat a brother or sister with contempt, or how can the gospel message and hatred coexist in the same heart? Furthermore, the meaning of "neighbor" surpasses location and is extended to everyone whom a believer encounters, as well as those who are potential recipients of love. For this reason, Jesus instructed his disciples to love their enemies, since it removes animosity as well as the resistance that formerly excluded others from receiving the benefits of redemption.[c]

The Lord, in fact, extends love even to those who are actively persecuting, for they too are sons of the heavenly Father and share in the same blessings. Therefore, categories such as neighbor and enemy, good and evil, and just and unjust cease, since the same sun and rain falls on everyone, as if the creator does not distinguish between those who are worthy of love. The Teaching pursues a similar objective, for Jesus did not differentiate between Jew or Gentile, because both are beneficiaries of divine favor. To make this point more evident, he separated the notion of love from its application, for such a distinction was not possible if the gospel objective was to bear witness to everyone encountered along the way. Paul the

---

[a] Hillel, a native of Babylonia, is considered the greatest sage of the Second Temple period, as his title *Zaken*, "the Elder," indicates. While he spent his early years in Jerusalem under the instruction of Abtalion and Shemaiah, his teachers, it was reported that he belonged to the house of David. Hillel was appointed "nasi" in 30 BCE and died when Jesus was a teenager (c. 10 CE). The elder was known for his seven hermeneutical principles that became the standard for interpreting the Torah for over a century. A spiritual revolution occurred under his influence, for his views were adopted gradually over several generations.

[b] Matthew 22:36-40. In reply to the inquiry involving which is the greatest commandment of the law, Jesus said, "You shall love the Lord your God with all your heart, and with all your soul, and with all your mind. This is the great and first commandment." The corollary ordinance is closely related, "You shall love your neighbor as yourself. On these two commandments depend all the law and the prophets."

[c] Matthew 5:43-48. This passage addresses Jewish oral law in which a neighbor and enemy are compared. Jesus instructed his disciples to love their enemies and to pray for their persecutors, because God does not show partiality in judgment. The remaining statement follows the Teaching very closely, including its use of the term "Gentiles" in the same context.

apostle was trained in the school of Hillel and was a convert to the faith after relentless hatred of believers and becoming their first official persecutor. Of all those who the Jerusalem community encountered, certainly he should receive enmity, and yet because of love he became the greatest herald of the faith among the Gentiles, those he was initially inclined to despise.

Paul adopted the same mandate and added, "Love does no evil against one's neighbor, for love is a fulfillment of the law."[44] While Pharisees,[45] the religious party to which he belonged, divided the Torah into various ordinances under similar headings, the Teaching identifies love as the basis for proper relationship with deity, society, community, and family. This is summarized in the single command, "Love your neighbor," that is, everyone in need of redemption, "as you love your own soul." This was a new ordinance directed equally to Jews and to Gentiles.[46] However, the audience intended for the Teaching was seeking understanding, whether they formerly belonged to Jewish, Hellenistic,[47] or Eastern tradition. As a result, this moral maxim of love is related to the law of reciprocity, often called the Golden Rule, and entails treating others in the same manner as one wants to be treated. This principle was well represented in the ancient world, with numerous variants in literary cultures.

The rule developed in the West, beginning with the words of Isocrates (436-338 BCE), "Do not do to others that at which you would be angry if you suffered it from others."[48] While various versions circulated in Hellenistic centers, the Jews of the Diaspora were taught a form that Hillel regarded as a fundamental tenet of his school, "What is hateful to you, do not unto your neighbor; this is the whole Torah, and all the rest is its commentary." Hillel

---

[44] Romans 13:9-10. The apostle lists a few commandments for his summary, in particular loving one's neighbor, for the purpose of the law was to fulfil that directive, and that means doing no wrong to another. This Paul addresses throughout this particular epistle.

[45] The Pharisees were the most prominent Jewish religious and political sect of the Second Temple period. The name designated those who were "separated" by their ascetic religious life in support of the oral law, that they claimed originated with Moses. Most were considered the successors of Ezra when these traditions. The Pharisees emerged after the Hasmonean revolt (165-160 BCE) in response to the Saducean control over the synagogue and Temple worship. The scribes and Pharisees labored together to interpret the law, both written and oral, the latter of which was compiled in the Mishnah and similar religious texts. They believed in resurrection of the dead, immortality of the soul, day of judgment, reward and retribution in the next life, the coming of Messiah, existence of angels, and other influential doctrines.

[46] Romans 3:29-30. Paul points out that the Lord is not only God of the Jews; he is also God of the Gentiles. This is because there is only one God, and he is encountered only by means of faith.

[47] The term "Hellenism" refers to the influence of Greek culture and literature on non-Grecian people. It was the product of Alexander the Great's expansion of his empire throughout the Mediterranean world. His death in 323 BCE resulted in several independent states unified with a common language. One of the consequences was an increase in commerce and in the exchange of goods and ideas. The effects of Hellenism were especially felt among the highly educated, such as those in government, art, education, or literature. It was Syrian Hellenism that led Antiochus IV to impose paganism on the Judean Jews, and Hellenism provoked tension among those living in the first century. In fact, by the birth of the church, Hellenistic Judaism was at odds with Pharisaic Judaism throughout Judea and the empire.

[48] Nicocles 61. Isocrates (436-338 BCE) was a celebrated Greek rhetorician and one of the ten renowned Attic orators. He is counted among the most influential scholars of his day and wrote extensively. He made a significant impact on the social and political dialogue of Greece, partially due to his notions of democracy. Isocrates was closely associated with Socrates, and in 392 he established a school of rhetoric and charged high rates from his students in order to guarantee their success. His rival was Plato, for he likewise founded an academic institution and traveled widely as a philosopher.

died when Jesus was a teenager, so this proverb was well represented among the Pharisees by the launch of his ministry. Consequently, when summarizing the main theme of scripture he stated, "Whatever you wish that men may do to you, thus also you shall do to them, for this is the law and the prophets."[49] In essence, he taught the apostles that undergirding the entire Jewish legal system was a principle of reciprocity that was widely embraced in regions where they were commissioned to preach the gospel.

In the East, five centuries earlier, a form of this proverb circulated widely among the teachings of Confucius (550-480 BCE), "Do not to others what you would not wish done to you." At its core, the principle was applicable across national and cultural borders, as seen in the system of Buddha, who expressed the same sentiment, "What is displeasing and disagreeable to me, how could I do it to another?"[50] Numerous forms also made their way into the religious and philosophical schools in antiquity, for its genius was simplicity. Hence, it is not surprising that a similar concept was taught in Hinduism, "One should never do to another that one regards as injurious to one's self. This, in brief, is the rule of dharma."[51] No matter the road traveled, whether east or west, or the form encountered, whether tradition or folktale, this was a common moral thread integrated into ancient cultures regarding the treatment of one's neighbor. It is not extraordinary, therefore, that the Teaching includes this tenet of the faith; in fact, it sets the tone for the entire treatise.

Loving one's neighbor takes on several forms, and abundant examples are provided throughout scripture and in the literature of early Jewish and Christian writers; however, it is introduced in this context with three types: moral, civil, and legal. This well-known saying of Jesus is condensed in the following manner, "If anyone gives you a slap on the right cheek, you turn to him also the other, and you will be fully developed. If anyone requisitions you one mile, you go with him two. If anyone removes your cloak, you give him also the tunic." Regardless of popular interpretation, this is not a call to passive resistance or a plea to personal abuse. This passage is placed in the context of loving one's neighbor, and it essentially provides a concise definition by means of three examples. The noun used for "slapping" can also refer to hitting with a club, rod, or whip, but since it is applied to the face the only possible meaning is "slap." The saying, however, is about the victim's response, for it did not result in serious damage and hence implies an insult rather than an injury.

For that reason, the saying mentions the other cheek, since the measured response was love, while the natural reaction was eye-for-eye, tooth-for-tooth retaliation, even for a minor

---

[49] Matthew 7:12. The gospel writer couched this saying between contrasting a human father with the heavenly Father and how he supplies good gifts to his children, especially to those who ask him. Therefore, whatever a man desires another to do, that individual should also do. The next statement is a return to the two ways axiom, "Enter by the narrow gate, for the gate is wide and the way is easy that leads to destruction, and many are those who enter by it."

[50] Samyutta Nikaya 55.7. The Samyutta Nikaya, "Connected Discourses," is a collection of sayings that comprise Buddhist scripture. Fragments have survived in Sanskrit and in a Tibetan translation. It is part of a much larger canon of scripture.

[51] Mahabharata, Anusasana Parva 113:8. The Mahabharata is a significant Sanskrit epic of ancient India. The narrative relates to the Kuruksetra War, and it contains both philosophical and devotional material. Among its most enduring portions is the Bhagavad Gita, a principal work popular in Indian religion. Its present form, as a compendium of treatises, scholars assign to the fourth century BCE. It is the longest epic poem that survived antiquity and is roughly ten times longer than the Iliad and the Odyssey combined.

infringement.[52] In this context, the believer seeks a more conciliatory resolution, the moral high ground, and therefore he consents to absorb the first insult without retribution in the hopes of restoring relationship. It does not anticipate a second or third strike, and it certainly is not condoning abuse or pious passivity. This is why there is an instructive rejoining phrase, "and you will be fully developed," for this suggests an adult rather than a childlike reaction. In the same respect, the principle contrasts love with the law, for the Jews upheld a detailed system with multiple layers of remuneration for every possible offense. The reference to the "right" cheek implies a backhanded strike, so while it may seem like a minor infraction, such offenses were taken seriously in Jewish communities of the first century.

The second example regarding loving a neighbor concerns requisition and expresses civil love in the context of a believer's responsibility to the state. It refers to the right of soldiers and others in the military to compel a person to carry gear or baggage for the distance of roughly one mile. By the first century, it came to include an official summons for any specific task, including carrying another's crossbeam to a place of crucifixion, as depicted in the passion narrative with Simon of Cyrene.[53] When applied more broadly, however, its meaning connotes pressing someone into service, and that could pertain to numerous situations that are not necessarily military actions. The response again is measured, for love offers assistance without incurring injury. For example, the soldier does not require his gear to be carried to the frontlines of battle, and while one mile was expected, the second exceeded the command with an extra mile, thus demonstrating the meaning of neighborly love.

In essence, love is expressed when a believer goes beyond what is anticipated in civil service, and this requires a deliberate intent; no abuse is implied. In this context, love is contrasted to natural desire, for it wars against the soul and compels an individual to demand justice when only a minor infraction ensued. However, in order for restoration to occur, forgiveness must be offered, and that begins when a spiritual alternative is initiated. Whether a slap or a mile, the violation is minor compared to the benefit of restored love. Therefore, the Teaching encourages abstaining from any behavior that places obstacles along the way of life that might cause another to stumble. All the while, a believer is expected to endure the inconvenient infringements that others introduce as an opportunity to demonstrate love. This principle reflects the actions of the nascent Jerusalem community, unlike the final example involving the court system.

The final illustration expresses "love" in the context of a legal dispute, for it involves a conflict and a courtroom. In this particular case a believer lost a lawsuit and extended to his opponent more than what the judicial system required, since restitution was necessary. In

---

[52] This is known as the principle of retaliation, *lex talionis*, a code of justice that was applied in various forms in the Jewish legal system. The punishment precisely matches the crime. It is found in several ancient cultures, particularly Babylonia. At the time of Jesus, Roman law was moving toward monetary compensation, as was the case in most Jewish communities. It is also found in the Code of Hammurabi, which precedes Mosaic law by roughly half of millennium, according to Rabbinic tradition (Leviticus 24:19-21). The oral form maintains five layers of compensation: pain, damages, medical expenses, incapacitation, and mental anguish.

[53] Simon of Cyrene was the man whom Roman solders compelled to carry the cross beam (patibulum) of Jesus along the designated course to the place of crucifixion, as reported in the synoptic gospels. He was from northern Africa in eastern Libya, where 100,000 Jews settled during the early years of Ptolemy's reign (323-285).

the first century, Jewish men of means generally wore three layers of clothing whenever displaying wealth or social status in public. The innermost garment was closest to the body and was made of a cotton or linen-like material. Alone, this simple attire took the form of a nightshirt that reached below the knees. It was unseemly to wear it alone and was considered "undressed." The second layer was a tunic or coat drawn tightly around the body with two sides overlapping each other and the garment bound at the waist with a belt or sash. These were generally worn together when a man appeared in public, whether at work, in the synagogue, or at home. It was the tunic of Jesus for which the soldiers cast lots in the Fourth Gospel.[54]

This third layer was comprised of a cloak, and this outermost vest was distinguished for its greater size and absence of a girdle. Scripture states that it could be offered as part of a pledge or oath but was to be returned by sunset. Reflecting a man's standing in the community and signifying dignity, culture, and distinction, it was often a sign of the priestly, educated, wealthy, or official class. Wearing this outer attire was regarded full-dress, so losing it in court meant that the defendant was pronounced guilty of not performing some sort of contracted task. There is no actual harm anticipated in this account, since both men were wealthy and the verdict was largely symbolical. Therefore, love is expressed in a legal repayment that involves damages incurred, even if the charge was false. The measured response on this occasion involved relinquishing a second layer of clothing when only one was compulsory. Paul instructs his congregations never to go to court in such a manner, especially against a fellow believer.[55]

All three responses were deliberate and varied based on the particular situation that arose, and each expressed love of one's neighbor. If the choice is between life and death, then rebirth is the result of dying to something, and in this case it is retaliation of the eye-for-eye variety, since the context is abstaining from fleshly and bodily desires. Love is more than a natural reaction, for it requires a spiritual element to guarantee that no further abuse occurs. Rational retribution cannot achieve love, and that is the intent of these three examples. The same principle was applied to alms,[56] for while believers are required to give freely to others,

---

[54] John 19:23-24. The tunic, or seamless robe of Jesus, has provoked innumerable legends and traditions, including a few associated with prominent places such the Cathedral of Trier. The Fourth Gospel states that the soldiers who crucified Jesus also cast lots for his tunic since it was woven from a single piece of cloth. Helena, Constantine's mother, is said to have discovered the tunic in the Holy Land in the year 327 or 328 along with several other relics. It was reputedly given to the city of Trier, where Constantine formerly resided.

[55] 1 Corinthians 6:1-8. The apostle instructs the church at Corinth not to go to court before the unrighteous, since they cannot judge justly, at least with regard to cases between fellow believers. After all, the pious will judge the world, he asserts; therefore, if possible, take all such matters directly to those involved, or before leaders of the church, who are wise and prepared to make sound decisions. In essence, Paul orders members not to expose such lawsuits, since love will find a way to resolve them, after it becomes the standard employed.

[56] Alms, or acts of charity on behalf of the poor, were common in ancient Israel, even though there is no term for the practice in Hebrew scripture. At the time of Jesus, however, the giving of alms had already become institutionalized and was considered to be one of the three main acts of piety, the other two being prayer and fasting. The New Testament contains several references to charitable acts performed on behalf of those in need; it was central to the gospel message. Many who joined the church sold their possessions and gave alms to assist poor women, orphans, and the disenfranchised. However, no compulsion was used; every good deed was to come from a heartfelt love for those who were assisted. The epistles of Paul contain numerous references to charitable donations given to the poor, and he instructed his churches to support the poor in Jerusalem when establishing a rule that a collection be taken on their behalf each Sunday. By the middle of the second century,

it was imperative to guarantee that responses corresponded to needs. In this respect, it was not just about being generously charitable but about accomplishing the most from an opportunity. If the recipient had a need, believers were to assist as much as possible; however, a penalty was compensated if no need existed and a member of the community still received.

Most early believers were drawn from the lower classes, so residual money was difficult to obtain and the need was generally met precisely, that is, in terms of specific food, clothing, shelter, and the like. The rule, apparently attributed to an apostle, is preserved, "Your alms shall sweat in your hands until you know to whom you give them." The interpretation is anticipated, for response to a need that involved money was tendered in the form of a coin, one unlikely as much as a denarius, since it purchased a full day's supply a bread. The monetary denomination mentioned is a quadrans, the smallest amount, since all expressions of love of any quantity accomplish the gospel mandate to give to those in need. Furthermore, if everyone in the community maintained this precept there would be a surplus for those who lacked. Hence, alms were based on necessity not on money, and later in the Teaching specific types of offerings are outlined in the form of "first fruits."

The next section of the Teaching expands this principle with practical applications of love. In this regard, the catechism offers advice regarding various opportunities to embrace apostolic tradition. Early church leaders taught that true piety was expressed from the heart rather than from defining the nuances of its function in the form of written laws or regulations that govern human behavior. While the Decalogue was retained, its meaning was applied more broadly in order to include Gentile matters, since they were the intended audience of the document. Consequently, it was reinterpreted in light of the gospel message and was heard in house churches that early believers attended. Among the topics included, under the heading of erroneous affection, are adultery, pedophilia, and sexual immorality, for they do not promote the well-being of victims or perpetrators. The same was applied to abortion, exposure, and infanticide, for the extermination of life in any form was defined as "murder" in early patristic literature.[57]

In this respect, adultery is described as misguided affection, pedophilia as prohibited affection, and immorality as devalued affection, each of which was defined based on the customs of first-century Greco-Roman culture, since such behavior was already proscribed

---

the church sustained an impressive voluntary system of collection for the poor and needy, without the notion of tithing or earthly benefits guaranteed the giver in return.

[57] Abortion was common in ancient Greece and Rome. Several motives compelled it, but the two most recurring incentives were poverty and the concealment of illicit sexual relations. Another strong impetus for women to have abortions was the preservation of their figures or youthfulness. Thus, abortion thrived, but not without some legal restrictions; the first occurred in 81 BCE, and it was intensified over the next three centuries. Doctors, pharmaceutical dealers, and abortionists were each able to perform them, while gynecologists or medical professionals might recommend different compositions for those medicinally induced. Most of the surgical techniques were primitive. Hippocrates (469-399 BCE), the father of medicine, from whose name the famous medical ethical oath derived, opposed abortion, as did all others in his guild. In contrast, exposure was an accepted practice in many centers of the ancient world; it involved leaving unwanted newborns in clay vessels on the side of the road or in a designated area of the city at the mercy of animals and the hostility of the climate. Motives for exposing a child varied greatly, including poverty, deformity, illegitimacy, vanity, and fear of childbirth. While many infants died, women who were unable or unwilling to bear children retrieved a few fortunate infants. Some of those rescued were raised as slaves for domestic and foreign purchase; others were cultivated to be gladiators in the arena or to be prostitutes for the many brothels of Rome.

in the Torah. The same applies to murder, for it is expanded to include potential children in the womb, abandoned children in the streets, and murdered children for the sake of convenience. Gentile converts to the faith were expected to cherish infants as much as their own lives, as is the mandate of the gospel. This sort of redefining of relationships was expected of married couples as well, for there is no closer neighbor than a wife or a child, and thus the governing principle of love is extended to sojourners, servants, and even hired workers. A household functioned as an extended family, in and out of the church, and that is what permitted their unique understanding of brotherly love.

Since love is not expressed in duplicity, apostolic instruction specified verbal responses and activities that damage relationships. Following the commandment, believers were not to desire the possessions or relations of others, since that sort of passion does not result in integrity or convey the love of a neighbor. The Teaching likewise defines transgressions of speech, such as breaking an oath, offering false testimony, speaking ill of another, misrepresenting true verbal intent, and failing to follow through with publicly made assurances and statements. The document opposes double-mindedness, for "the tongue is a trap of death"; therefore, every spoken word should be truthful and fulfilled in action, rather than false or empty. Believers are not to devise wicked schemes against others or to hate anyone, but some they should correct and for others they should pray, because loving a neighbor should occur even at the expense of one's own pride.

Consequently, the catechism instructs the faithful to avoid those who act contrary to the way of life or to possess such a character. However, apostolic tradition was less concerned with sin than with its origins and causes, and seven examples are offered, such as: anger leads to murder, desire leads to sexual immorality, divination leads to idolatry, lying leads to theft, and complaining leads to blasphemy. Each type of sin can be prevented, since each is the result of choices made in sequence and therefore involves human impulses or inclinations. Furthermore, two of these transgressions are counted among the commandments in the Torah; hence, the explanation for catechumens served as a commentary. To prevent murder do not be inclined to anger, but also do not promote one's views without taking those of others into consideration. Do not cause strife or contention as if encouraging partisanship rivalry, and do not be irascible to the point of irrational assault. Similarly, to avoid adultery, the apostles taught how to control sexual desires, bridle abusive and suggestive speech, as well as exchange lewd and suggestive glances for those expressed in fidelity and integrity.

The remaining five examples are equally effective to demonstrate that sin can be avoided, for it is not a product of human nature but of human endeavor. Sin requires deliberate choices in the same manner as the path that leads to life. Since it fosters an attitude that thrives in arrogance and self-deceit, the Teaching encourages believers to associate instead with righteous and humble individuals. In essence, behavior worthy of a catechumen is established as gentleness, patience, mercy, and innocence. Underlying the ethical principle of love is acknowledging that nothing exists apart from God, so believers are encouraged to receive as beneficial whatever happens and to realize that for every path heading to death there is another leading to life. This is not to suggest that the early church developed a form of fatalism but that a righteous person can learn from every life event without necessarily understanding its ultimate purpose at the time. For this reason, the catechumen was instructed to search daily for other believers in order to find comfort in their words, especially those more experienced in the faith.

In an egalitarian society like the nascent Jerusalem church there was little tolerance for arrogance, for everyone was a servant and that required a form of humility that exalted even the most pitiful among them. While united in purpose, the community was comprised of different voices, and each was to be heard without fomenting division. Those who quarreled were expected to reconcile, and no one was to show favoritism when exposing sin through confession, regardless of office, social status, or duration of membership in the church. The commandments of the Lord were to be applied properly without rigorous legalistic displays. Each new member protected the instruction received as a catechumen without editing its content or augmenting it with additional regulations. The community was primarily comprised of families, and hence, a brief statement about children is included regarding raising them in the faith, both sons and daughters.

The same was the case for servants of the wealthy, for they were not to be commanded in harshness, since they likewise believed in the same God, who rules similarly over their masters. The Teaching consistently reminds the newly converted that there is no favoritism in the eyes of God, and they were to model this perspective as equals in the kingdom. Similarly, household domestics among the rich were to behave to the same degree as they submit to the Lord. The treatment of indentured workers was addressed in the epistles of Paul; in fact, that was the primary reason for this correspondence to Philemon.[58] Every believer is comparably bound to the Lord and thus is to despise hypocrisy and to protect the integrity of the gospel message without adding or taking away from it. Transgressions against all others were publicly confessed in each house church in order to guarantee full recovery and restoration. This resulted in prayer with a clean conscience and closes the description of the "way of life."

A CHURCH INITIATION

Justin was the most renowned second-century apologists. He was born at Flavia Neapolis (Shechem) in Samaria around 114 and died at Rome under Marcus Aurelius between 162 and 168. He was a devout student of philosophy and retained that professional attire after conversion. He traveled widely as a teacher before settling in the capital, where he addressed two prominent apologies on behalf of the church to Antoninus Pius and the Roman senate. Later patristic writers claim that he wrote numerous documents, some of which are preserved only in fragments. In pursuit of what he identified as the true philosophy of

---

[58] The Epistle to Philemon is a correspondence that Paul and Timothy sent, but it was essentially a private letter. The recipient sponsored a house church, and the content concerns one of his slaves named Onesimus, who made his way to the apostle but was returned with a letter urging kindness and clemency. Philemon was a citizen of Colossae; his fugitive servant was from Phrygia. There is a suggestion in the brief letter that he robbed Philemon before leaving, but since then he had become a believer through Paul's efforts. This is the briefest of apostle's epistles and is generally assigned to 58 or 59.

Christ, Justin composed treatises in opposition to major heretical movements as well as to pagan religion and practice. He was an original thinker, the most influential writer between Paul and Origen, and was the first to cloak Christian thought in philosophical terminology. A thorough description of a Sunday service in the capital was recorded in his apology in the year 165, many aspects of which seem to originate in the Teaching.

A new believer is baptized after he has acknowledged our teaching. We escort him to the place where those identified as brothers are assembled. They offer sincere prayers in common for all who are baptized as well as for others wherever they may dwell. This is observed so that through our actions we may be counted worthy to become good and esteemed citizens as well as observers of the ordinances, now that we have learned the truth and have attained eternal salvation at last. After all prayers are finished, we greet one another with a kiss, and at that time the bread and cup of wine, blended with water, are brought to the one presiding over the brothers. Once received, he pronounces praise and glory to the Father of all things through the authority of the Son and of the Holy Spirit. The one presiding then recites lengthier prayers of thanksgiving to God on behalf of all who were deemed worthy to receive such benefits. When these prayers and thanksgivings are completed, all those present express their approval by saying *Amen,* a word that means "so be it" in the Hebrew language.

After the one presiding has celebrated the Eucharist and all those present have expressed their assent, men who we call deacons distribute to those present elements of bread and wine mixed with water. Over them a prayer of gratitude is spoken so that they may partake. Afterwards, the deacons deliver the remaining elements to those who were absent from the celebration. We call this food the Eucharist, and of it no one is permitted to consume except those who believe in the veracity of our teaching, those cleansed through baptism for the remission of sins and are thus regenerated, and those who live according to the principles that Christ established. We do not receive these elements as common bread or drink but as symbolizing Jesus Christ our Savior, who became human through the logos of God and possessed both flesh and blood for our salvation. We were instructed that this food is blessed through reciting his words, for by this means our blood and flesh are nourished, and this occurs through its assimilation and represents both the flesh and blood of Jesus, who became incarnate. ...

On each Sunday those who live in the cities or in outlying districts gather in a common assembly. The memoirs of the apostles or the prophetic writings are then read as long as time permits, and after the reader finishes, the one presiding instructs us verbally and invites all who gathered to imitate these examples of virtue. We then all rise in unison and offer prayers. ... The one who presides also utters prayer and thanks, according to his ability, and the people express their approval and say, amen. The elements are then distributed to those in attendance and are consumed, and the remains are sent through the deacons to those absent.

If they are willing, the wealthy contribute whatever amount they find appropriate, and this collection is deposited with the one presiding. With these funds he assists the orphans and widows, those who are deprived due to illness or to any other cause, those in prison and visitors sojourning among us; in short, he takes care of all those in need.[59]

The Teaching instructs the reader not to stray from its directives but instead strive for greater capacity, especially if its contents prove to be difficult. The intent was to cultivate spiritual growth, a popular metaphor in early church literature. Therefore, after instructions concerning the ways of life and death, that summarizing the sayings of Jesus around the notions of love and respect, the Teaching includes a vice list containing most sins a first-century catechumen could imagine. This catalogue of offenses likely overwhelmed the initiate with a sense of legalism, a form most commonly attributed to Pharisaic oral tradition. However, this inventory of iniquity merely establishes how love is not manifested, for a greater principle offers relief and perspective. In a single sentence a believer's responsibility is individually assessed: "If you can bear the whole yoke of the Lord, you shall be perfect." This is a daunting statement, partly due to the nature of the allegory introduced.

Such a yoke was used to join two field animals around the neck so that they could work in harmony at the will of the farmer. If anyone was so yoked to the Lord, that is, acts according to his will like a foreman in the field, such a worker is perfect. As translated, however, this last word is problematic, since the English notion of *perfect* is not equivalent to the Greek meaning. It refers instead to being diligent to the end of a particular a task; in essence, it connotes reaching the full potential of one's ability. As a result, the first part of the statement reads, "If you are able to bear the yoke of the Lord, you will reach the maximum of your potential." This is the same terminology used in the synoptic tradition, "Be *perfect*, as your heavenly Father is *perfect*."[60] The actual meaning is, "You should live to the utmost of your ability in the same manner as your heavenly Father." Jesus instructed his disciples to put all they had into what they did, and the Teaching insists that new believers to do the same.

The second layer of this metaphor, however, contains a remarkable supposition, "If you are able to bear the yoke of the Lord, you will reach the maximum of your potential, but if you cannot do this, do what you are able." What relief this must have provided to the Jewish teachers of the catechism, for it echoed very few elements of Pharisaic legalism. It offered, instead, a practical morality based on individual growth under the guidance of the human conscience and the indwelling Spirit of God. The path toward spiritual maturity is therefore cultivated in daily life as one's potential is expanded together with the community in an atmosphere of love, respect, and encouragement. The date of composition is suggested

[59] Justin, 1 Apology 65-67. These chapters from the apology reflect many of the practices described in the Teaching; in fact, there is enough similarity to suggest that Justin was familiar with the catechism. The depiction of the church service as well as the agape meal and Eucharist are particularly analogous.

[60] Matthew 5:48. The context for this passage is loving your neighbor, for rather than hating your enemy believers love and pray for those who persecute them. Anyone can love those who return the sentiment, but genuine love exceeds beyond that shared in common, whether culture, province, or custom (5:43-48).

in the closing line of this section, for it involved food laws as well as each believer's responsibility prior to the apostolic council in Acts 15, when meat offered to idols was ultimately addressed. The conference occurred in the year 50 and was convened in Jerusalem.

The second portion of the Teaching describes early church practice in the form of applied catechetical principles. Perhaps the most interesting aspect of this section is not what it contains but what it omits. The new convert was baptized at the end of his instruction, for it was the act of initiation into the community of believers. Baptism was not unique to Christianity, however, it was the final requirement for Gentile proselytes in Judaism and was especially popular in the Hillelian school. The custom was a rite of purification by means of water, and as an ablution such acts were required of all holy item. Such a notion of "holy washing" was attached to baptism. For early Christians, it began with John the Baptist, who introduced a new form of repentance, a cleansing of the heart, in preparation for the kingdom of God. The baptism of Jesus launched his ministry, and it was the same that the twelve disciples performed in the Jordan shortly after John was arrested.

The modes of baptism described in the Teaching include immersion and sprinkling, but the main form was by affusion,[61] a pouring over the head usually while standing in water. Baptism was symbolic, and that is why the preference was to use a flowing spring rather than the warm water of a public bath. Part of the ritual involved the recitation of applied content that espoused basic instruction in the Jesus movement, for it was essential that a catechumen understood this body of material prior to membership. After discussing this process, the Teaching describes fasting and prayer as practiced in the congregation. The Pharisees maintained certain days and encouraged them in local synagogues; the early believers likewise retained this custom but altered the days on which they occurred to reflect the betrayal and crucifixion of Jesus. Attached to fasting was prayer, as often was the case, according to contemporary Jewish literature, for it distinguished between its pious and wicked forms.

Prayer was perceived as a spiritual bridge between humans and their Maker, who both hears and responds to the righteous. Consequently, it took on many forms: confession, petition, meditation, thanksgiving, praise, adoration, supplication, intercession, and even worship, both liturgical and personal. Access to God through the Holy Spirit resulted in prayer, and this was accomplished by means of faith, the intent of which was to determine divine will for each believer. It is not surprising, then, that the Teaching preserves the earliest form that Jesus taught his disciples. The chief components of the Lord's Prayer were acknowledging the Creator, whose name is to be uttered with respect and whose reign is embraced as a reality. Believers were to follow the instruction of Jesus to live day-by-day expecting

---

[61] Affusion was a method of baptism in which water was poured on the head; hence, the Latin term means "to pour on." This likely had its origins in the anointing of kings, and hence, to enter the kingdom of God it became an essential act. It was one of four modes of baptism in the early church; the others were immersion, submersion, and aspersion (or sprinkling). It is first mentioned in the Teaching, and water was poured out on the head three times, likely while standing in a stream or river, as was the custom that John the Baptist introduced. This is implied in the phrase "in living water," that is, running water and fresh when available. Those baptized in prison prior to martyrdom were only able to use affusion, and the same was true of the infirmed or dying. Finally, the baptism of the Holy Spirit was poured out (Acts 2:17-18, 33); the same was said of Peter's encounter with the Gentiles at Caesarea (10:45-47).

the Lord to supply their needs. If they wanted to be forgiven, they likewise were required to forgive others.[62]

One intent of daily prayer was deliverance from the evil one, who opposes the purposes of God and of his people. This is particularly evident in the version of the Lord's Prayer preserved in the Teaching, for it predates the form canonized in the synoptic gospels. A definitive sign that the document is early is its final line, "Pray in this manner three times a day." This demonstrates that members of the community maintained the three hours of prayer observed among the Jews but changed its content in order to reconcile the message of Jesus with the customs of the local church. As a catechism, instruction in the Teaching prior to baptism closed with a simple statement, "This is the way of life." All that proceeded defined the narrow path to righteousness; in contrast was the broad road leading to death and destruction. Baptism was regarded as a seal against mortality and as a mark of commitment to the community of believers. This was not a threat, veiled or overt, for the anticipated consequences of sin were death; therefore, it awaited everyone equally.

The early church message was not based on fear or dread but on opportunity and hope, for immortality was extended to those willing to embrace its benefits. Instruction for the catechumen, therefore, resulted in new life that reflected the teachings of Jesus as understood through the messianic purpose of overcoming death and providing relief from sin and shame. When everyone in the community implemented this theology, it fostered a familial environment, one conducive not only to confession but also to cultivating trust and acceptance. Believers were bound to weekly oaths of purity, and the Teaching states that they occurred on each Lord's Day, when the faithful assembled to eat a common meal and to confess sins. The same custom was observed in Paul's churches, for they offered similar acknowledgment so that prayers remained pure and were uttered with a clean conscience. However, rather than seek absolution from the clergy, it was offered from the community as a means of restoring members to a state of innocence required to partake of the Eucharist.

Baptism was linked to confession in the first century, for it implied that all offensive behavior ended after initiation into the local community of believers. This "cleansing" was attained by means of forgiveness,[63] and it reflected the sinless objectives of each member. In addition to an initial acknowledgment of faith; therefore, specific subsequent confessions provided continued development of character on a path to spiritual maturity. For each initiate, this process began at baptism. This notion is likewise maintained in the Teaching, and that is what, in part, makes it an important contribution to early church studies with regard to behavior expected of each believer. It was assumed that no sin would be committed after

---

[62] Forgiveness, as a concept, developed in Jewish scripture; it presumes that only by divine intervention can sin be removed. The offender was expected to repent, which often involved an expressed intention not to repeat the transgression. Hence, forgiveness carried the idea of restoration to the position one occupied prior to committing the sin. Its significance took on a new dimension in Christianity, one based on atonement through the blood of Jesus and upon his teaching on the subject. The basic underlying meaning was the complete removal of the causes of offense; that is, sin was taken out of the way, whether a debt, trespass, or iniquity.

[63] 1 John 1:9-10. The Fourth Gospel concurs, for the writer asserts that if a believer confesses his sin, the Lord is faithful and just to forgive the iniquity in order to cleanse all forms of unrighteousness. However, if anyone says that he has not sinned, that person makes God a liar and is spiritually bankrupt. The term *forgive* in this context, therefore, suggests the removal of sin, no matter its form.

baptism, as witnessed clearly in the Shepherd of Hermas,[64] a popular allegory that addressed a single question: does one sin after baptism prevent an individual from immortality. This explains the numerous references to "cleansing waters" in early church literature.

Another illuminating description in the Teaching involves worship, since it contains the most primitive form of liturgical prayer. The cup, in this account, was blessed first and then the bread. Jesus is then proclaimed to belong to the vine of David. Simple thanks was offered, for this was implied in the meaning of "Eucharist," a sacred meal commemorating the death and resurrection of Jesus. Only baptized members were permitted to partake, for they understood its symbolism and significance. The ceremony continued with an agape meal, and the prayers used on that occasion are included in the Teaching. The clergy attended and administered this commemorative meal, and over time it developed into standardized rituals with regional customs. By the middle of the second century, the congregation participated in the spoken liturgy and specific roles were assigned to the laity with special prayers and blessings used throughout the celebration.

No minister earned a salary in the early church, not even apostles or prophets, and if any leader asked for money he was removed from office and labeled a false teacher. Support for the nascent church was voluntary and was donated "without compulsion," as Tertullian wrote at the close of the second century.[65] A nearly identical view was portrayed in other early patristic writers, as corroborated in dozens of documents. However, the contribution was not usually offered in the form of money but from one's livelihood, a portion of which was given to assist others in need. The term used, "first fruit,"[66] draws from the concept of a designated portion of the agricultural crops mentioned in the Torah; later it was employed metaphorically in the New Testament.[67] As a result, while believers supported the community from their occupations, it was only from the first portion of their produce. The intended recipients included the sick, poor, widows, orphans, and deprived in their neighborhood.

---

[64] Hermas was author of the Shepherd, a Christian allegory from the sub-apostolic age. He was likely a freedman who was married with children, but he was later persuaded to practice abstinence. The Muratorian Fragment asserts that he was the brother of Pius, bishop of Rome, who died in 154. Hermas was a church reformer, but nowhere does he claim to be a prophet, although he approached the subject often. Since all of its visions were written in the form of a Jewish apocalypse, with the presence of a revealer and mysterious disclosures that need to be explained, it is certain that Hermas was familiar with the literature of that genre. The Shepherd reads like a persecution document and it likely circulated around 140. Due to popularity, it was attached to Codex Sinaiticus.

[65] Tertullian was the first great apologist and theologian of the Latin-speaking church. He was born at Carthage in the middle of the second century and died there between 220 and 240. He received an excellent education in jurisprudence and rhetoric and he wrote fluently in Greek and Latin. Tertullian was a lawyer in Rome prior to his conversion in 197. He was the most voluminous writer in early Latin Christianity and led the defense against Marcion and the Gnostics. His ascetic lifestyle prompted the scholar to address a number of treatises on morals, discipline, and on various aspects of Christian conduct. Tertullian was intrepid, precise, and witty. He was a master of sarcasm and was an original thinker.

[66] First fruits in Judaism connoted a portion of the agricultural crops, the first-ripe grain and fruit, to be offered to the Lord in thanks for a bountiful harvest. The underlying principle was that the firstborn belongs to God, whether human, animal, or vegetable. The Israelites presented them to the priests on the eighth day, the day on which believers also met for worship and to present their gifts (Teaching 13). First fruits implies the hope of abundance, especially in Paul's epistles, for he taught that the Lord offered to humanity a first fruit in the Holy Spirit as a pledge of greater blessings in the future, chief among them was resurrection.

[67] For example: Exodus 23:19, Leviticus 23:10, Proverbs 3:9, Ezekiel 44:30, and Romans 11:16. It was this secondary meaning that the editor of the Teaching had in mind.

There was no infrastructure to support, since believers met in homes, so all that remained were those marginalized in society or those destitute of means. This was a universal practice in the faith and it was one of the defining factors that resulted in increased membership through the close of the second century. Addressing the Roman emperor at that time, the founder of Latin theology expressed,

> The approved men of our elders preside over us, and they obtained that honor not by purchase but by established character. There is no buying and selling of any sort in the things of God. … On the monthly day, if he wishes, each contributes a small donation, but only at his pleasure and only if he is able for there is no compulsion, all is voluntary. These gifts … are not taken from there and spent on feasts, carousing, or restaurants, but to support and to bury poor people, to supply the wants of boys and girls destitute of means and of parents, and of the aged confined to the house, or those who suffered shipwreck, and those in the mines or banished to the islands, or shut up in the prisons for nothing but their fidelity to the cause of God's church.[68]

This custom was understood as applied love of one's neighbor, for it extended to the most desperate as well as the wealthiest among them.

Early church leadership was comprised of specific full and part-time clergy with an extensive laity cooperating in the service of the community. The apostles delivered the oral gospel and recalled traditions transmitted from the founding years of the faith, while the prophets exhorted its interpretation, expounded the scriptures, and spoke on behalf of the Lord. Evangelists preached the message of redemption in specific unchurched regions, as the shepherds, or pastors, were local ministers of its principles and of its application. Teachers instructed the community from the depths of their understanding and traveled extensively throughout the Greco-Roman world. Locally, elders guarded the integrity of the gospel and directed the congregation based on experience and insight, while presbyters made up a local council to resolve conflicts and to assist in governance. Deacons served the congregation and fed the hungry, clothed the ill-clad, and housed the homeless, and the entire community was comprised of saints, that is, those consecrated to represent the church by means of righteous behavior.

The most significant office, according to the Teaching, was apostle, and those who operated in this capacity were commissioned with authority to act as ambassadors; however, the term could refer to an individual or to a group.[69] Their general function was to represent and

---

[68] Tertullian, Apology 39. Tertullian wrote from Carthage a few decades after Justin was active in Rome, and he describes several of the same customs and practices. This includes elders presiding over the agape meal and the way in which money was collected on a specific day of the month to bury the poor, to supply the needs of orphans, to assist those confined in a house, to care for those who suffered shipwreck, or those forced to work in the mines, those banished to the islands, or those locked up in prison simply for remaining faithful to the gospel.

[69] Paul, however, maintained that prophecy was the most desirable spiritual gift in his treatment of the topic in 1 Corinthians 14. This is because he understood the role of prophet as one who encourages and strengths the church; hence, it benefits the entire congregation, in contrast to other offices, such as apostle. For

to deliver messages with official sanction, even though it could vary depending on the mission. Jesus chose twelve among his hundreds of followers, and what distinguished them was disciples were hearers of a master, while apostles carried out his directives. The number twelve corresponded to the tribes of Israel, for Jesus was portrayed as a new patriarch and fulfiller of an ancestral promise. As initial leaders of the church, they traveled beyond the environs of Judea prior to setting out on missionary journeys throughout the Roman empire. As they prepared to depart, others were appointed to the office in a secondary capacity, such as Paul,[70] who commissioned others for his ministry twenty years after the founding the Jerusalem community.

It is this second generation of apostles that the Teaching describes, for they ministered at home and abroad as they established house churches throughout the Greco-Roman world. This stage of church organization occurred roughly a dozen years after the initial communities of Judea were founded. No matter their authority, apostles were not to remain more than two or three days at any single location and they could never request financial support. As Paul taught his congregations, the foundation of the church was built on apostles and prophets who labored together on behalf of believers scattered throughout a Christian diaspora. Akin to their function were the prophets, charismatic individuals endowed with receiving and imparting revelation. They did not choose their profession but were selected as vessels of disclosure who uttered inspired words and interpretations. The message delivered was based on the premise that God discloses his will over successive generations by means of profound mysteries.

The term "prophet," therefore, connotes standing in place of another to speak. It did not necessarily involve, or require, predicting the future but a reality in the present. For the early church, the behavior of Jesus was the criterion used to identify the true from false prophet, and Paul described how many in his churches sought earnestly to prophesy. The Teaching depicts their function in the church as central to its purpose, and the mysteries associated with them were seldom challenged. In the same respect, every prophet was tested to guarantee the genuineness of his appointment, and like the apostles none was paid for services rendered. This detail is especially important, since they were recipients of the local first fruits, that is, the donations of various kinds gathered for distribution to the poor, to the helpless, to the imprisoned, and to the infirmed.

The third tier of clergy, as represented in the manual, was the teacher, like those who served in the synagogue. Many arose among Pharisaic converts, such as Paul the apostle, and established the basic tenets of the faith as well as their application. Some were resident in communities, while others traveled extensively from town to town expounding the gospel

---

this reason, Paul listed the functions according to authority: apostles, prophets, teachers, and those operating within the body of believers (1 Corinthians 12:28). He likewise maintained that the church was established on the foundation of apostles and prophets (Ephesians 2:20), for the Spirit of God directs their endeavors (3:5) as demonstrated in the gifts that each brings, whether apostles, prophets, evangelists, pastors, or teachers (4:11).

[70] Paul admits this in his Corinthian correspondence when saying that Jesus first appeared to Cephas and then to the twelve, after which more than five hundred people saw him resurrected, before James the Just witnessed the event. Last of all, the apostle says, Jesus appeared to him, "for I am the least of the apostles, one unfit to be called an apostle, since I persecuted the church" (1 Corinthians 15:3-9). Paul clearly drew from sources to which the gospel writers were not privy.

message and proclaiming the messianic kingdom. Even though the Teaching places them after the apostles and prophets, they were distinct from the local overseers and deacons who served solely in the churches to which they were appointed. Due to the honor of the office, a special warning was attached to teachers, especially in light of Jesus challenging the pretense of the Jewish scribes. False teachers were a constant problem, especially those who desired to break away and to found their own brand of the faith. Therefore, safeguards were instituted to protect believers, and this took the form of thoroughly evaluating them prior to instructing the congregation.

This responsibility also fell on the catechumens, for they were to recite authentic apostolic tradition prior to full admission into the local church. They were directed to retain only that received during instruction and nothing that was contrary to the two ways section of the Teaching. If the message diverged from apostolic tradition, a teacher was marked as false and removed from the congregation for correction or reprimand. In contrast, genuine teachers were welcomed, fed, clothed, and housed after they were examined, but they likewise were to remain no longer than a day or two, unless they decided to dwell permanently among the believers. The same policy applied to traveling Christians, for they were initially received, but after few days it was expected that they would continue as sojourners or acquire an occupation and contribute to the community. If they refused to comply, they were confronted for taking advantage of the generosity of the faithful and for refusing to obtain gainful employment.

The resident clergy was trained to intercede when this sort of conduct arose, and that included overseers and deacons who served on the Lord's Day as well as throughout the week. They are described in the Teaching as gentle men who were not avaricious; they instead were truthful in what they said and approved in the behavior they exhibited. They performed the liturgy and organized the charity work in the community with the local laity, who likewise contributed to the weekly gatherings. One of their principal duties was to maintain unity and to intervene with those who quarrel or create dissension. The body of believers also assisted in this task, for they were commanded not to speak with those who refused to correct abuse such as displays of angry and divisive language. This served as a warning against the rise of deceptive claims from those intent on destroying the integrity of the church.[71]

APOCALYPTIC WARNING

The Roman community suffered oppression from state-sponsored persecution and remained hidden from the public. Its leaders were not inclined to cower from the pursuit of those determined to dismantle the church and to harass its members. This is exhibited in a prayer preserved in the earliest Christian document composed from the capital. The writer

---

[71] Matthew addressed this issue and concluded that if a brother sins against another, expose his offense between the two of them, but if he does not cooperate then take one or two other believers with to confront him, since it takes two witnesses to confirm such behavior. However, if he refuses to listen, inform the leaders of the church, and if he still neglects to repent, treat him as a Gentile and a tax collector (Matthew 18:15-17).

was Clement of Rome, and he addressed the Corinthians forty years after Paul dispatched his letter to correct certain anomalies that arose. He reminds them of his mentor's words, for a similar issue involving the clergy reemerged in the same community. His epistle was read like scripture for half a century, as demonstrated in Codex Alexandrinus,[72] for it was appended to that manuscript together with other documents from the same era. His prayer on behalf of the first-century world is preserved in this text.

Grant us, O Lord, the ability to set our hope on your name, the source of all creation, and open the eyes of our hearts so that we may know you, the one who alone abides highest in the lofty and holy in the holy, the one who lays low the insolence of the proud, who scatters the imaginings of nations, who sets the lowly on high and brings the lofty low, who makes rich and makes poor, who brings death and causes life, who alone is the patron of spirits as well as the God of all flesh, who looks into the abysses, who scans the works of men, the helper of those who are in peril, the savior of those who are in despair, the creator and overseer of every spirit, the one who multiplies the nations upon earth and has chosen from humanity those who love you through Jesus Christ, your beloved Son, through whom you instructed us, sanctified us, and honored us.

We beseech you, Lord and Master, to be our helper. Save those among us who face trials. Have mercy on the lowly, lift up the fallen, be shown unto the needy, heal the ungodly, convert the wanderers of your people, feed the hungry, release our prisoners, raise up the weak, comfort the faint-hearted. Let all the nations know that you alone are God, that Jesus Christ is your Son, and that we are your people and the sheep of your pasture. Through your design the everlasting fabric of the world was manifested.

You, Lord, Creator of the earth, are faithful throughout all generations, are righteous in your judgments, are marvelous in strength and excellence, are wise in creating and prudent in establishing what you have made, for you are good in the things that are seen and faithful to those who trust you, are merciful and compassionate; forgive us our iniquities, our poor choices, transgressions, and shortcomings. Do not hold the sins of your servants against them, but wash us with the cleansing of your truth; guide our steps to walk in holiness, righteousness, and singleness of heart, and teach us to do that which is good and well pleasing in your sight and in the eyes of our government.

Lord, shine your face upon us in peace for our benefit, so that your mighty hand may shelter and deliver us from every sin by your uplifted arm. Deliver us from those who hate us wrongfully. Extend unity and peace to all those who

---

[72] Cyril Lucar, patriarch of Constantinople, brought Codex Alexandrinus to England and presented the manuscript to Charles I in 1628, seventeen years after the publication of the King James Bible. The trustees of the British Museum produced a full photographic facsimile of the fifth-century codex. It is the work of five different scribes and begins with Matthew 25:6; it is a complete text, except for John 6:50-8:52 and 2 Corinthians 4:13-12:6. The epistle of Clement and a homily in his name are also attached to the manuscript. Alexandrinus measures 32.1 cm. x 26.4 cm. and contains 773 vellum leaves with 46 to 52 lines to the column.

dwell on the earth, for you likewise gave it to our fathers when they called on you in faith and truth with holiness, so that we may be saved, while we render obedience to your supreme and excellent name and to our rulers and governors upon the earth. You, Lord and Master, have given them the power of sovereignty through your excellent and unspeakable might, for we know the glory and honor that you gave so that we may submit to them and resist your will in nothing.

Grant unto them, therefore, O Lord, health, peace, unity, and stability, that they may administer the government that you gave them without failure. For you, O heavenly Master and King of the ages, give to humanity glory and honor and power over all things that are upon the earth. Lord, direct their counsel according to what is good and well-pleasing in your sight, so that they may administer in peace and gentleness with godliness the power that you have given them, so that they may obtain your favor.

You, who alone are able to do this and things far greater, we praise through the high priest and guardian of our souls, Jesus Christ, through whom is all glory and the majesty unto you both now and for all generations and forever. Amen.[73]

What enabled this eloquent prayer was a belief that Jesus would return soon to end the present age and to usher in a new era of peace and serenity as part of an eternal redemptive plan of the Lord.

Apocalypticism was a unique worldview that emerged in Judaism during the Hellenistic period and was highly developed by the first century. It blended prophetic literary images with foreign influences, especially those adopted during the Persian exile. It was a unique Jewish phenomenon that provided a solution to the discontinuity of the messianic promise of an eternal Davidic kingdom ruling over Israel. Principal features included a dualistic struggle between light and darkness, the activity of angels and demons, a dividing of history into epochs, the belief in resurrection, and heavenly journeys during which secrets of creation and the world-to-come were disclosed. Instead of looking back over history, apocalypticism reinterpreted it in order to breathe new meaning into scripture; in essence, it turned history into prophecy. The final section of the Teaching contains a warning that describes various signs that suggest the end of the age and the *parousia*.

This worldview provided a way for devout Jews to cope with reality of life under Rome by offering a meaningful framework within which they could decide how to respond to their pagan environs. Those who embraced this perspective distinguished between "this world" and the "next world," and this included popular notions such as the "end of days." Such an

[73] 1 Clement 59-61. Clement of Rome was a leader and scribe in Rome during the last decades of the first century. His epistle is the earliest surviving document from the capital. More literature was circulated in his name than in any other non-biblical character of the Ante-Nicene era. His letter reached an almost canonical status and was attached to a few biblical manuscripts. It was composed at the close of the first century, 95-96, and in it he cites Paul and describes events in the apostle's life that no other writer of his period preserved, including his release from prison after a second trial and his missionary activity in Spain. Clement's epistle was found in the same codex that contained the Teaching; in fact, its discoverer, Bryennios, published the first complete text of these correspondences in 1875, prior to the catechism in 1883. The previous form was preserved in Codex Alexandrinus, but it was tattered in places and peppered with lacunae.

interpretation explained events in a cosmic process accompanied by upheavals in nature that resulted in a final conflict between rival spiritual forces. However, this worldview cannot be identified with a single social movement or strand of theology, for it was manifested in diverse literary endeavors, and some of these documents influenced the New Testament writers. Early believers were convinced of this description of the world, and its images are replete throughout the synoptic tradition. However, the second-century apologists especially adopted this interpretation of the last days, as did the apostolic fathers before them.

The Teaching contains the earliest summary regarding the end of the age attributed to the apostles and of the signs and events expected to unfold before the Lord's return. While it provided consolation to believers, some of whom experienced persecution, the warning also instructed believers to be prepared, for no one knows for certain when these events will occur. The faithful were encouraged to meet frequently and to labor diligently on behalf of each other, for life is most meaningful when individuals are living to the maximum of their capacities during the last days. It was expected that at the end of the age deception would increase like never previously in history, so it was important to remain vigilant. During this time, some believers will dramatically change in behavior, while others who formerly loved will only hate. As conditions worsen, a few will join the ranks of those who persecute, arrest, and imprison believers, as Jesus likewise declared in the synoptic gospels.[74]

At this time, a world deceiver will arrive in the political arena, and he will convince those unaware that he is the long-awaited savior. He accomplishes this through signs and wonders that he performs as if he were the messiah. This implies that some who were formerly devout will misinterpret the phenomena he displays. As a means of warning, the Teaching asserts that the entire human race will face a horrific and catastrophic testing of its resolve. The campaign is effective enough to cause some believers to abandon the cause, while those who remain faithful during persecution will ultimately find salvation. Three signs will usher in the final days: the clouds will open, the sound of a trumpet will blast, and the dead righteous will resurrect to join Jesus upon his return. Every early patristic writer taught that persecution, perhaps even the tribulation, was necessary to occur, for it separates the faithful from the fraudulent believer.

The apostles were told that each of them would suffer and die and that the world would hate and despise them. They were therefore instructed to be persistent in duty and attentive in watch. As martyrs, the twelve, together with a host of additional church leaders, acknowledged that no one could escape persecution in the last days. In essence, it became

---

[74] Matthew 24:3-14. Matthew's parallels to this apocalyptic pericope are stunning. "The apostles asked him, When will this come to be, and what will be the sign of your coming and of the end of the age? Jesus then replied, Listen, so that no one leads you astray, for many will appear in my name saying, I am the Christ, and they will lead many astray. You will hear of wars and rumors of wars; make sure that you are not alarmed, for this must occur, but the end has not yet arrived. Nation will rise against nation and kingdom against kingdom, and there will be famines and earthquakes in various places. All this is but the beginning of birth-pangs. They then will deliver you up to suffer and to be executed, and all nations will hate you for my name's sake. Many will then fall away and betray one another and hate one another. Many false prophets will arise and lead many astray. Since wickedness is multiplied, most men's love will grow cold, but the one who endures to the end will be saved. This gospel of the kingdom will be preached throughout the whole world as a testimony to all nations, and then the end will come." The word "nations" may also be translated "Gentiles," which in this context makes more sense due to the nature of the proclamation.

fuel for apocalyptic fires to blaze in the street, in the marketplace, and in the surrounding villages. What made their efforts successful were hearts yearning for an imminent *parousia* and the end of the age. Only then could a new era be inaugurated in which the faithful are rewarded and the fallen martyrs are extolled. Beginning with Nero, when edicts were first passed against believers, persecution intensified and the members of the community grew more confident that the final signs were about to appear. This worldview suggests a very early age of the Jesus movement, one prior to the death of the apostles, the destruction of the Temple, and the expansion of the church to "the end of the earth."

MATTHEW 24	TEACHING 16
Take heed that no one leads you astray.	You shall be alert on behalf of your life; your lamps shall not be extinguished and your waists shall not be ungirded, but you shall be ready, for you do not know the hour in which our Lord comes.
Many will come in my name saying, "I am the Christ" and will mislead many. You will certainly hear of wars and rumors of wars; see that you are not frightened, since it is necessary to happen, but the end is not arrived. Nation will be raised against nation and kingdom against kingdom, and there will be famines and earthquakes in many places, but all these things are a beginning of *end-time* woes.	
They will then deliver you to affliction and will kill you, and all the nations will hate you because of my name. Many will then be caused to fall away and will hand over *to prison* one another and will hate one another.	The creation of humans then shall enter into the fiery ordeal of examination, and many shall be caused to fall and shall be destroyed, but the one who is accursed shall save those who remain in their faith. When the lawlessness then increases they shall hate and shall persecute and shall hand over each other,
Many false prophets will be raised and will cause many to wander, and because of the increased lawlessness, the love of many will grow cold.	In the last days, then, the false prophets and corrupters shall be multiplied, and the sheep shall be changed into wolves, and the love shall be changed into hate.

However, the one who endures to an end, this one will be saved. This gospel of the kingdom will be proclaimed in all the inhabited earth for a testimony to all nations, and then the end will come.

Therefore, when you see the detestable thing causing the desolation, that was spoken through Daniel the prophet, stand in a holy place (the reader should understand). Those who are in Judea should flee to the mountains, the one on the housetop should not come down to take things out of his house, and the one in the field should not turn behind to take his cloak. Woe to the pregnant women and to those who are nursing, in those days. Pray that your flight may not occur in winter nor on a Sabbath, for there will be great affliction, such as has not happened from the beginning of the world until now, neither by any means may *ever* happen. Except those days were shortened, no flesh would be saved, but on account of the chosen those days will be shortened. If anyone then says to you, "Look, here is the Christ," or, "Here *he is*," do not believe. False christs and false prophets will be raised, and they will perform great signs and marvels so as to lead astray, if possible, even the chosen. Behold, I have told you beforehand; therefore, if they say to you, "Look, he is in the desert," do not go out; *if they say* "Look in the private rooms," do not believe. As the lightning comes from the east and shines unto the west, so will be the *parousia* of the Son of man. Wherever may be the carcass, there the eagles will assemble. Immediately after the affliction of those days, the sun will

You then shall be frequently gathered together striving for the things that are proper for your souls, for the whole time of your faith shall not benefit you, except you may be made complete in the last time.

and then the world deceiver shall appear as a son of God, and he will perform illicit things that has never been out of an age.

and he shall perform lawlessness that has never been out of an age.

and he shall perform signs and wonders, and the earth shall be given over into his hands,

---

be darkened, the moon will not give her light, the stars will fall from heaven, and the powers of the heavens will be shaken.

The sign of the Son of man will then appear in heaven, and all the tribes of the land will greatly mourn. They will see the son of man coming on the clouds of heaven with power and great glory, and he will send his angels with a loud trumpet, and they will assemble his chosen out of the four winds, from one end of the heavens to the other.

The signs of truth shall then be revealed: first a sign of an opening in heaven, next a sign of a trumpet's sound, and third a resurrection of those who are dead, but not of all, but like it was said, "The Lord shall come and all the holy ones with him." The world then shall see the Lord who comes above the clouds of heaven.[75]

SUMMARY AND INTENT

Since the Teaching was primarily intended for first-century proselytes to the faith, it is not surprising that portions of its text may have been adapted from similar synagogue and church manuals. This may also explain its double title, the latter of which adds the phrase "to the Gentiles." The Christianized form was edited and attributed to the twelve apostles, based partly on instruction that was later integrated into the synoptic tradition. It was then expanded with ordinances regarding baptism, fasting, and prayer as well as the Eucharist and the agape meal. Its two ways section initially circulated independently, the opening line of which was borrowed from the Torah,[76] and was blended with genuine sayings, whether of Jesus or of the twelve.[77] The main topics involve portions of the Decalogue, and this may explain its authoritative tenor. The injunction about being yoked to the Lord may be an allusion to the two types of proselytes in ancient Judaism: the one who accepts all the laws of the Torah and the one who only embraces the Noachian laws. Nonetheless, there is no doubt that its present form was edited for Gentile converts to the church, even if its core ethics are Jewish in origin.

---

[75] The Teaching 16:1-8. This comparison between the Teaching and the Gospel of Matthew shows that they either borrowed from the same sources, edited some independent tradition attributed to the apostles, or the latter made use of the former. Their views on the *parousia* and kingdom of God likewise contain numerous parallels, as if the gospel writer represents a later age of the same school of thought.

[76] Deuteronomy 6:5, Leviticus 19:18. While based on the Torah and known as the great commandment, this statement contains Jesus' summary of Jewish law as preserved in the synoptic tradition (Matthew 22:35-40, Mark 12:28). It was paraphrased from the Torah and was provided in response to a legal question asked concerning the ordinances of Moses.

[77] Matthew 5:39-48, Luke 6:27-39. These parallel passages are attributed to Jesus in the gospels but to the apostles in the Teaching. Both contain the lesson of loving your neighbor as one's self and turning the other cheek, which in Matthew's account is closely akin. The main differences include "sinners" in place of "Gentiles" and the closing line regarding "perfect," which in Luke is rendered "merciful." This is a superb example of how these two traditions utilize the "Q" document, since each addressed a specific individual or community of believers.

The Teaching was compiled during a stage in church history when persecution was anticipated but not fully realized. This restricts its date prior to the reign of Nero, who died in June 68. Since the document implies that the twelve apostles are active in the church and that the Jerusalem Temple is still standing, an era before the emperor's reign of terror is expected. Its perspective about the end of the world, its unguarded language and unsophisticated style, its primitive description of church ritual and practice, and its transitory depiction of clerical offices each points to a much earlier date. Since the Teaching reads like a catechism intended for Gentile converts to the faith, it must be assigned to a time when the first significant influx of non-Jewish believers occurred but before the year 50, the year of the apostolic council. At that time, the Jesus movement was still indebted to an oral form of the gospel, as preserved among the apostles, and apparently, one might say certainly, before the synoptic accounts circulated.

Since there is no mention of Paul or even a hint of his theological system, the manual must date near the beginning of his ministry, since he was the great champion of Gentile admission into the church. The role for the clergy, and the various function each serves reflects a period of transition, like that described occurring in the Antiochene community, when Peter reported to the Jerusalem leadership the emergence of Gentiles in local congregations.[28] Furthermore, readers are identified as members of "the Way," and multiple modes of baptism are employed. The Teaching is written with few references to Jesus; in fact, its Christology is implied rather than explained. This certainly suggests the earliest stage of the gospel message, prior to any written form that has survived, when its content was primarily a collection of Jesus sayings with limited narrative. If this is sufficient as evidence, it appears that the catechism dates between 45 and 51, and that renders it among the earliest surviving documents of the church.

---

[28] Acts 11-13. Peter's report to the church at Jerusalem, under the direction of James the Just, affirms that Gentiles initially received the gospel along the coast in Joppa and Caesarea. However, it was Antioch that made the greatest gains, so Barnabas was sent to investigate, and he took Paul with him. Both were commissioned to preach to these non-Jewish converts, and this became the origin of Paul's mission.

APPENDIX A

A LITERAL TRANSLATION OF THE TEACHING
FROM THE ORIGINAL GREEK TEXT

Brent S. Walters

THE TEACHING OF THE TWELVE APOSTLES
A Teaching of the Lord through Twelve Apostles to the Gentiles

Two Ways (1:1-3). There are two ways, one of life and one of death, but *there is* a great difference between the two ways. The way of life, therefore, is this: first, you shall love God who made you, secondly, your neighbor as yourself, and all things whatever, if you desire them not to happen to you, you also shall not do them to another. Of these words then the teaching is this: you shall bless those who are cursing you and you shall pray for your enemies and you shall fast for those who are persecuting you, for what benefit is it if you shall love those who are loving you? Do not even the nations do the same? However, for you, you shall love the one who hates you and you shall not have an enemy.

Expressing Love (1:4-5a). You shall abstain from fleshly and bodily desires. If anyone may give you a slap on the right cheek, you shall turn to him also the other, and you shall be mature. If anyone may requisition you one mile, you shall go away with him two. If anyone may remove your cloak, you shall give him also the tunic. If anyone may take away from you what is yours, you shall not demand it back, for you are not even able. You must give to everyone who is asking you, and you must not demand it back, for the Father wills that we give to everyone out of our own freely given gifts.

Giving Alms (1:5b-6). Fortunate is the one who gives according to the commandment, for he is innocent. Woe to those who are receiving, for, if on the one hand, anyone who has a need is receiving he is innocent; on the other hand, if anyone has no need he shall pay a penalty concerning why he received and for what purpose, and once in prison he shall be examined concerning what he did, and he shall not come out from there, not until he has given back the last quadrans. However, also concerning this it has been said, "Your alms shall sweat in your hands until you may know to whom you may give."

Destructive Behavior (2:1-2a). However, a second commandment of the teaching: you shall not murder, you shall not commit adultery, you shall not sexually corrupt boys, you shall not practice sexual immorality, you shall not steal, you shall not practice magic, you shall not mix potions, you shall not murder a child by an abortion nor put to death one that has been born.

Being a Neighbor (2:2b-7). You shall not desire the things of your neighbor. You shall not break oaths, you shall not give false testimony, you shall not speak evil, you shall not resentfully bear a grudge. You shall not be double-minded nor double-tongued, for the double-tongue is a trap of death. Your word shall not be false or empty but fulfilled in action. You shall not be one who takes advantage, or a robber, or a hypocrite, or spiteful, or arrogant. You shall not devise a wicked scheme against your neighbor. You shall not hate anyone, but the one you shall correct, for the other you shall pray; the other you shall love more your own soul.

Overcoming Sin (3:1-6). My child, you shall flee from every wicked person and from everyone of a same nature. You shall not be inclined to anger, for anger leads to murder, or a partisan or quarrelsome or irascible, for from all these murders are produced. My child, you shall not be given to sexual desire, for sexual desire leads to sexual impurity, or a foul-mouthed person or a lifter-up of the eyes, for from all these adulteries are produced. My child, you shall not be an augur, since it leads to idolatry, or an enchanter or an astrologer or one who performs purification rites or wish to see these things, for from all these idolatry is produced. My child, you shall not be a liar, since it leads the one lying into the act of stealing, or a lover of money or conceited, for from all these thefts are produced. My child, you shall not be a grumbler, since it leads to being a slanderer, or stubborn or evil-minded, for from all these blasphemies are produced.

Seeking Maturity (3:7-10). However, you shall be gentle, for those who are gentle shall obtain the earth. You shall be patient and merciful and innocent and quiet and good and one who trembles at every word that you heard. You shall not consider yourself better nor shall you give arrogance to your soul. Your soul shall not be joined with the haughty, but with righteous and humble men you shall be associated. You shall willingly receive as good things the happenings that occur to you, since you know that nothing comes into existence apart from God.

Daily Commitment (4:1-4). My child, may the one who is speaking to you the word of God be remembered night and day, and you shall honor him as a lord, for from where the dominion is spoken about there is a lord. You shall search daily among the faces of the saints so that you may find comfort in their words. You shall not desire division but you shall reconcile those who are quarreling. You shall judge justly; you shall not receive favoritism to expose transgressions. You shall not doubt whether it shall be or not.

Ransom for Sins (4:5-8). You shall not, on the one hand, be one who extends the hands to receive; on the other hand, be one who retracts them to give. If you hold with your hands you shall give a ransom for your sins. You shall not hesitate to give nor while you give shall you complain, for you shall know who is the good paymaster of the reward. You shall not be one who has turned away the needy but one who shall share all things with your brother, and you shall not contend that it is your own, for if you are partners in immortal things how much more in the mortal things?

Children and Servants (4:9-11). You shall not lift up your hand from your son or from your daughter, but from their youth you shall teach the reverence of God. You shall not command your slave or maid-servant in your harshness, those who are hoping on the same God, lest they not revere the God over you both, for he does not come to call toward favoritism but over those whom the Spirit has prepared. However, you slaves are subjected to your lords as an image of God in modesty and reverence.

Confession and Integrity (4:12-14). You shall hate all hypocrisy and all that is not pleasing to the Lord. On the one hand, you may not abandon the commandments of the Lord; on the other hand, you shall protect what you received since nothing has been added or taken away. In a house-church you shall confess your transgressions, and you shall not engage in your prayer with an evil conscience. This is the way of life.

Way of Death (5:1-2). However, a way of death is this: first of all it is wicked and full of curse, murders, adulteries, sexual desires, prostitutions, thefts, idolatries, magic arts, chemical arts, robberies, false testimonies, hypocrisies, duplicity, deceit, arrogance, depravity, stubbornness, greediness, a foul-mouth, jealousy, shamelessness, pride, pretension, persecutors of the good who hate truth, who love a lie, who do not know a reward of righteousness, who are not attached to the good or to righteous judgment, who stay awake not for the good but for the wicked, who are far away from gentleness and patience, who are lovers of worthless things, who pursue retribution as reward, who have no mercy on a beggar, who do not labor with those oppressed, who do not know the one who created them, murderers of children, corrupters of that God formed, who turned away from the needy, who are mistreating the afflicted, mediators of the rich, lawless judges of the poor, who are filled with sin; may you be rescued, children, from all of these.

Procuring Perfection (6:1-2). You shall see that no one may cause you to wander from this way of the teaching, since he is instructing you outside of God, for if, on the one hand, you are able to carry the whole yoke of the Lord you shall be fully developed, but if, on the other hand, you are not able what you are able this you shall do.

Food Laws (6:3). Concerning food, you shall endure what you are able, but you shall pay special attention to meat offered to an idol, for it is worship of dead gods.

Waters of Initiation (7:1-3). Concerning the baptism, after all these things are done you shall baptize in this manner; you shall baptize into the name of the Father and of the Son and of the Holy Spirit in living water. If, however, you may not have living water, you shall baptize into other water, and if you are not able in cold *then* in warm. If, however, you may not have either, you shall pour out water onto the head three times into *the* name of Father and of Son and of Holy Spirit.

Days of Fasting (7:4-8:1). However, before the baptism the one baptizing and the one being baptized shall fast beforehand and any others if they are able, and command the one being baptized to fast one or two *days.* However, your fasts shall not be with the hypocrites, for they are fasting to second and to fifth of sabbaths, but as for you, you shall fast on fourth and preparation.

Daily Prayer (8:2-3). You shall not pray like the hypocrites but like the Lord commanded in his gospel; in this manner you shall pray: our Father, who is in heaven, your name shall be made holy, your kingdom shall come, your will shall come to be as in heaven and upon earth; you shall give to us our bread for our need today, and you shall forgive us our debt as also we are forgiving our debtors, and may you not bring us into a trial, but you shall rescue us from the wicked one, since it is your might and glory into the ages. You shall pray three times of the day in this manner.

The Eucharist (9:1-5). Concerning the Eucharist, you shall give thanks thus: first concerning the cup, "We give thanks to you, our Father, on behalf of the holy vine of David your child, whom you made known to us through Jesus your child; to you the glory into the ages." Concerning also the fragments, "We give thanks to you, our Father, on behalf of the life and knowledge that you made known to us through Jesus your child; to you the glory into the ages. As this which is the fragment, while scattered upon the hills yet brought together became one, so the church shall be brought together from the limits of the earth into your kingdom, because yours is the glory and the power through Jesus Christ into the ages." However, in no way shall anyone eat or shall drink from your Eucharist, except those who have been baptized into the name of the Lord, for also concerning this the Lord said, "You may not give the holy thing to the dogs."

Agape Thanks (10:1-6). After you are satisfied, you shall give thanks thus: "We give thanks to you, holy Father, on behalf of your holy name that you caused to dwell in our hearts, and on behalf of the knowledge and faith and immortality that you made known to us through Jesus your child; to you is the glory into the ages. You, Master all-powerful, created all things because of your name; you gave food and also drink to humanity for enjoyment in order that they all may give thanks, but to us you freely gave spiritual food and drink and eternal life through your child. Before all things we give thanks to you because you are powerful; to you is the glory into the ages. You shall remember, Lord, your church, to deliver her from all evil and to make her complete in your love, and you shall bring her together from the four winds, she who has been made holy, into your kingdom that you have prepared for her, since to you is the power and the glory into the ages. Grace shall come and this world shall pass away. Hosanna to the God of David. If anyone is holy, he shall come; if anyone is not, he shall repent; maran atha, amen."

Prophetic Prescript (10:7). However, you shall allow the prophets to give thanks as much as they wish.

Itinerant Teachers (11:1-2). Whoever then arrives may teach you all these things said beforehand; you shall receive him. However, if that teacher has turned he may instruct another teaching to abolish *these things*; you may not listen to him, but *if he teaches* to increase righteousness and knowledge of the Lord you shall receive him like the Lord.

Traveling Apostles (11:3-6). Concerning the apostles and prophets, according to the decree of the gospel thus you shall do. You shall welcome every apostle who comes to you like the Lord, but he shall not remain except one day, and if there is a need another also, but if he remains three *days* he is a false prophet. However, when departing the apostle shall receive nothing except bread, not until he may spend the night, but if he asks for silver he is a false prophet.

Genuine Prophets (11:7-12). You shall not put to the test nor shall you pass judgment on any prophet who speaks in a spirit, for every sin shall be forgiven but this sin shall not be forgiven. However, not everyone who speaks in a spirit is a prophet, but if he has the conduct of the Lord. From their behavior, then, the false prophet and the *true* prophet shall be known. Every prophet who appoints a table in a spirit shall not eat from it; otherwise, he indeed is a false prophet, and every prophet who teaches the truth if he does not what he teaches is a false prophet. However, every genuine prophet who has been examined, who is performing an earthly mystery for a church but is not teaching you to do how great he does, you shall not judge, for with God he has judgment, for in the same way also did the ancient prophets. However, whoever may say in a spirit, "You shall give me silver or something different," you shall not listen to him, but if on behalf of others who are in need he may say to give no one shall judge him.

Sojourn and Settling (12:1-5). You shall, however, welcome the one who comes in a name of the Lord but after you have examined him, for then you shall know since you shall have insight right and left. If the one who comes is traveling by you shall give assistance to him as much as you are able, but he shall not remain among you except two or three days, if there is a need. However, if he wishes to reside among you as an artisan he shall work and *then* he shall eat, but if he does not have a craft you shall provide according to your insight; by no means shall an unemployed Christian dwell with you. If, however, he wishes to do neither he is a Christ trafficker; you shall pay attention to such a kind.

First Fruits (13:1-7). However, every genuine prophet who wishes to reside among you is worthy of his food. In the same manner, just as the laborer, a genuine teacher is also worthy of his food. Therefore, after taking every first fruit of produce of a winepress and of a threshing floor, of oxen and also of sheep you shall give of the first fruits to the prophets, for they are your high priests. However, if you do not have a prophet you shall give to the poor. If you may make a batch of bread, while you take of the first fruit you shall give according to the commandment. In the same manner, while you take of the first fruit of a jar of wine or of oil that is opened you shall give to the prophets, and also while you take of the first fruit of silver and also of clothing and of every property, as seems *good* to you, you shall give according to the commandment.

The Lord's Day (14:1-3). However, during the Lord's Day of the Lord, while you are gathered together you shall break bread and give thanks, after you have confessed your transgressions so that your sacrifice may be pure. Hence, everyone who has a quarrel with his companion shall not be assembled together with you, not until he become reconciled so that your sacrifice may not be defiled, for this is what the Lord said, "In every place and time offer to me a pure sacrifice, because I am a great King, says the Lord, and my name is marvelous among the nations."

Resident Clergy (15:1-2). Therefore, you shall choose *by raising hands* overseers and deacons worthy of the Lord, men who are gentle and not greedy for money and truthful and approved, because to you they conduct a religious service, the liturgy of the prophets and teachers. Therefore, you may not despise them, for they are the honorable ones among you with the prophets and teachers.

Unity in Community (15:3-4). However, you shall correct each other not in anger but in peace, like you have in the gospel, and everyone who fails against another shall speak nothing and he shall not hear from you until he may repent. Thus, the prayers and alms and all activity you shall do like you have in the gospel of our Lord.

Apocalyptic Alertness (16:1-2). You shall be alert on behalf of your life; your lamps shall not be extinguished and your waists shall not be ungirded, but you shall be ready, for you do not know the hour in which our Lord comes. You then shall be frequently gathered together striving for the things that are proper for your souls, for the whole time of your faith shall not benefit you, except you may be made complete in the last time.

Signs of the End (16:3-8). In the last days, then, the false prophets and corrupters shall be multiplied, and the sheep shall be changed into wolves, and the love shall be changed into hate. When the lawlessness then increases they shall hate and shall persecute and shall hand over each other, and then the world deceiver shall appear as a son of God and he shall perform signs and wonders, and the earth shall be given over into his hands, and he shall perform lawlessness that has never been out of an age. The creation of humans then shall enter into the fiery ordeal of examination, and many shall be caused to fall and shall be destroyed, but the one who is accursed shall save those who remain in their faith. The signs of truth shall then be revealed: first a sign of an opening in heaven, next a sign of a trumpet's sound, and third a resurrection of those who are dead, but not of all, but like it was said, "The Lord shall come and all the holy ones with him." The world then shall see the Lord who comes above the clouds of heaven.

APPENDIX B

THE GREEK TEXT OF THE TEACHING OF THE TWELVE APOSTLES

ΔΙΔΑΧΗ ΤΩΝ ΔΩΔΕΚΑ ΑΠΟΣΤΟΛΩΝ

Διδαχὴ κυρίου διὰ τῶν δώδεκα ἀποστόλων τοῖς ἔθνεσιν.

CHAPTER ONE

1. Ὁδοὶ δύο εἰσί, μία τῆς ζωῆς καὶ μία τοῦ θανάτου, διαφορὰ δὲ πολλὴ μεταξὺ τῶν δύο ὁδῶν. 2. Ἡ μὲν οὖν ὁδὸς τῆς ζωῆς ἐστιν αὕτη· πρῶτον ἀγαπήσεις τὸν θεὸν τὸν ποιήσαντά σε, δεύτερον τὸν πλησίον σου ὡς σεαυτόν· πάντα δὲ ὅσα ἐὰν θελήσῃς μὴ γίνεσθαί σοι, καὶ σὺ ἄλλῳ μὴ ποίει. 3. Τούτων δὲ τῶν λόγων ἡ διδαχή ἐστιν αὕτη· εὐλογεῖτε τοὺς καταρωμένους ὑμῖν καὶ προσεύχεσθε ὑπὲρ τῶν ἐχθρῶν ὑμῶν, νηστεύετε δὲ ὑπὲρ τῶν διωκόντων ὑμᾶς· ποία γὰρ χάρις, ἐὰν ἀγαπᾶτε τοὺς ἀγαπῶντας ὑμᾶς; οὐχὶ καὶ τὰ ἔθνη τὸ αὐτὸ ποιοῦσιν; ὑμεῖς δὲ ἀγαπᾶτε τοὺς μισοῦντας ὑμᾶς, καὶ οὐχ ἕξετε ἐχθρόν. 4. ἀπέχου τῶν σαρκικῶν καὶ σωματικῶν ἐπιθυμιῶν· ἐάν τίς σοι δῷ ῥάπισμα εἰς τὴν δεξιὰν σιαγόνα, στρέψον αὐτῷ καὶ τὴν ἄλλην, καὶ ἔσῃ τέλειος· ἐὰν ἀγγαρεύσῃ σέ τις μίλιον ἕν, ὕπαγε μετ᾽ αὐτοῦ δύο· ἐὰν ἄρῃ τις τὸ ἱμάτιόν σου, δὸς αὐτῷ καὶ τὸν χιτῶνα· ἐὰν λάβῃ τις ἀπὸ σοῦ τὸ σόν, μὴ ἀπαίτει· οὐδὲ γὰρ δύνασαι. 5. παντὶ τῷ αἰτοῦντί σε δίδου καὶ μὴ ἀπαίτει· πᾶσι γὰρ θέλει δίδοσθαι ὁ πατὴρ ἐκ τῶν ἰδίων χαρισμάτων. μακάριος ὁ διδοὺς κατὰ τὴν ἐντολήν· ἀθῷος γάρ ἐστιν. οὐαὶ τῷ λαμβάνοντι· εἰ μὲν γὰρ χρείαν ἔχων λαμβάνει τις, ἀθῷος ἔσται· ὁ δὲ μὴ χρείαν ἔχων δώσει δίκην, ἱνατί ἔλαβε καὶ εἰς τί· ἐν συνοχῇ δὲ γενόμενος ἐξετασθήσεται περὶ ὧν ἔπραξε, καὶ οὐκ ἐξελεύσεται ἐκεῖθεν, μέχρις οὗ ἀποδῷ τὸν ἔσχατον κοδράντην. 6. ἀλλὰ καὶ περὶ τούτου δὲ εἴρηται· Ἱδρωσάτω ἡ ἐλεημοσύνη σου εἰς τὰς χεῖράς σου, μέχρις ἂν γνῷς, τίνι δῷς.

CHAPTER TWO

1. Δευτέρα δὲ ἐντολὴ τῆς διδαχῆς· 2. οὐ φονεύσεις, οὐ μοιχεύσεις, οὐ παιδοφθορήσεις, οὐ πορνεύσεις, οὐ κλέψεις, οὐ μαγεύσεις, οὐ φαρμακεύσεις, οὐ φονεύσεις τέκνον ἐν φθορᾷ, οὐδὲ γεννηθὲν ἀποκτενεῖς, οὐκ ἐπιθυμήσεις τὰ τοῦ πλησίον. 3. οὐκ ἐπιορκήσεις, οὐ ψευδομαρτυρήσεις, οὐ κακολογήσεις, οὐ μνησικακήσεις. 4. οὐκ ἔσῃ διγνώμων οὐδὲ δίγλωσσος· παγὶς γὰρ θανάτου ἡ διγλωσσία. 5. οὐκ ἔσται ὁ λόγος σου ψευδής, οὐ κενός ἀλλὰ μεμεστωμένος πράξει. 6. οὐκ ἔσῃ πλεονέκτης οὐδὲ ἅρπαξ οὐδὲ ὑποκριτὴς οὐδὲ κακοήθης οὐδὲ ὑπερήφανος. οὐ λήψῃ βουλὴν πονηρὰν κατὰ τοῦ πλησίον σου. 7. οὐ μισήσεις πάντα ἄνθρωπον, ἀλλὰ οὓς μὲν ἐλέγξεις, περὶ δὲ ὧν προσεύξῃ, οὓς δὲ ἀγαπήσεις ὑπὲρ τὴν ψυχήν σου.

CHAPTER THREE

1. Τέκνον μου, φεῦγε ἀπὸ παντὸς πονηροῦ καὶ ἀπὸ παντὸς ὁμοίου αὐτοῦ. 2. μὴ γίνου ὀργίλος, ὁδηγεῖ γὰρ ἡ ὀργὴ πρὸς τὸν φόνον, μηδὲ ζηλωτὴς μηδὲ ἐριστικὸς μηδὲ θυμικός· ἐκ γὰρ τούτων ἁπάντων φόνοι γεννῶνται. 3. τέκνον μου, μὴ γίνου ἐπιθυμητής, ὁδηγεῖ γὰρ ἡ ἐπιθυμία πρὸς τὴν

πορνείαν, μηδὲ αἰσχρολόγος μηδὲ ὑψηλόφθαλμος· ἐκ γὰρ τούτων ἁπάντων μοιχεῖαι γεννῶνται. 4. τέκνον μου, μὴ γίνου οἰωνοσκόπος, ἐπειδὴ ὁδηγεῖ εἰς τὴν εἰδωλολατρίαν, μηδὲ ἐπαοιδὸς μηδὲ μαθηματικὸς μηδὲ περικαθαίρων, μηδὲ θέλε αὐτὰ βλέπειν· ἐκ γὰρ τούτων ἁπάντων εἰδωλολατρία γεννᾶται. 5. τέκνον μου, μὴ γίνου ψεύστης, ἐπειδὴ ὁδηγεῖ τὸ ψεῦσμα εἰς τὴν κλοπήν, μηδὲ φιλάργυρος μηδὲ κενόδοξος· ἐκ γὰρ τούτων ἁπάντων κλοπαὶ γεννῶνται. 6. τέκνον μου, μὴ γίνου γόγγυσος, ἐπειδὴ ὁδηγεῖ εἰς τὴν βλασφημίαν, μηδὲ αὐθάδης μηδὲ πονηρόφρων· ἐκ γὰρ τούτων ἁπάντων βλασφημίαι γεννῶνται. 7. ἴσθι δὲ πράϋς, ἐπεὶ οἱ πραεῖς κληρονομήσουσι τὴν γῆν. 8. γίνου μακρόθυμος καὶ ἐλεήμων καὶ ἄκακος καὶ ἡσύχιος καὶ ἀγαθὸς καὶ τρέμων τοὺς λόγους διὰ παντός, οὓς ἤκουσας. 9. οὐχ ὑψώσεις σεαυτὸν οὐδὲ δώσεις τῇ ψυχῇ σου θράσος. οὐ κολληθήσεται ἡ ψυχή σου μετὰ ὑψηλῶν, ἀλλὰ μετὰ δικαίων καὶ ταπεινῶν ἀναστραφήσῃ. 10. τὰ συμβαίνοντά σοι ἐνεργήματα ὡς ἀγαθὰ προσδέξῃ, εἰδὼς ὅτι ἄτερ θεοῦ οὐδέν γίνεται.

CHAPTER FOUR

1. Τέκνον μου, τοῦ λαλοῦντός σοι τὸν λόγον τοῦ θεοῦ μνησθήσῃ νυκτὸς καὶ ἡμέρας, τιμήσεις δὲ αὐτὸν ὡς κύριον· ὅθεν γὰρ ἡ κυριότης λαλεῖται, ἐκεῖ κύριός ἐστιν. 2. ἐκζητήσεις δὲ καθ᾽ ἡμέραν τὰ πρόσωπα τῶν ἁγίων, ἵνα ἐπαναπαῇς τοῖς λόγοις αὐτῶν. 3. οὐ ποθήσεις σχίσμα, εἰρηνεύσεις δὲ μαχομένους· κρινεῖς δικαίως, οὐ λήψῃ πρόσωπον ἐλέγξαι ἐπὶ παραπτώμασιν. 4. οὐ διψυχήσεις, πότερον ἔσται ἢ οὔ. 5. Μὴ γίνου πρὸς μὲν τὸ λαβεῖν ἐκτείνων τὰς χεῖρας, πρὸς δὲ τὸ δοῦναι συσπῶν. 6. ἐὰν ἔχῃς διὰ τῶν χειρῶν σου, δώσεις λύτρωσιν ἁμαρτιῶν σου. 7. οὐ διστάσεις δοῦναι οὐδὲ διδοὺς γογγύσεις· γνώσῃ γάρ, τίς ἐστιν ὁ τοῦ μισθοῦ καλὸς ἀνταποδότης. 8. οὐκ ἀποστραφήσῃ τὸν ἐνδεόμενον, συγκοινωνήσεις δὲ πάντα τῷ ἀδελφῷ σου καὶ οὐκ ἐρεῖς ἴδια εἶναι· εἰ γὰρ ἐν τῷ ἀθανάτῳ κοινωνοί ἐστε, πόσῳ μᾶλλον ἐν τοῖς θνητοῖς; 9. Οὐκ ἀρεῖς τὴν χεῖρά σου ἀπὸ τοῦ υἱοῦ σου ἢ ἀπὸ τῆς θυγατρός σου, ἀλλὰ ἀπὸ νεότητος διδάξεις τὸν φόβον τοῦ θεοῦ. 10. οὐκ ἐπιτάξεις δούλῳ σου ἢ παιδίσκῃ, τοῖς ἐπὶ τὸν αὐτὸν θεὸν ἐλπίζουσιν, ἐν πικρίᾳ σου, μήποτε οὐ μὴ φοβηθήσονται τὸν ἐπ᾽ ἀμφοτέροις θεόν· οὐ γὰρ ἔρχεται κατὰ πρόσωπον καλέσαι, ἀλλ᾽ ἐφ᾽ οὓς τὸ πνεῦμα ἡτοίμασεν. 11. ὑμεῖς δὲ οἱ δοῦλοι ὑποταγήσεσθε τοῖς κυρίοις ὑμῶν ὡς τύπῳ θεοῦ ἐν αἰσχύνῃ καὶ φόβῳ. 12. Μισήσεις πᾶσαν ὑπόκρισιν καὶ πᾶν ὃ μὴ ἀρεστὸν τῷ κυρίῳ. 13. οὐ μὴ ἐγκαταλίπῃς ἐντολὰς κυρίου, φυλάξεις δὲ ἃ παρέλαβες, μήτε προστιθεὶς μήτε ἀφαιρῶν. 14. ἐν ἐκκλησίᾳ ἐξομολογήσῃ τὰ παραπτώματά σου, καὶ οὐ προσελεύσῃ ἐπὶ προσευχήν σου ἐν συνειδήσει πονηρᾷ· αὕτη ἐστὶν ἡ ὁδὸς τῆς ζωῆς.

CHAPTER FIVE

1. Ἡ δὲ τοῦ θανάτου ὁδός ἐστιν αὕτη· πρῶτον πάντων πονηρά ἐστι καὶ κατάρας μεστή· φόνοι, μοιχεῖαι, ἐπιθυμίαι, πορνεῖαι, κλοπαί, εἰδωλολατρίαι, μαγεῖαι, φαρμακίαι, ἁρπαγαί, ψευδομαρτυρίαι, ὑποκρίσεις, διπλοκαρδία, δόλος, ὑπερηφανία, κακία, αὐθάδεια, πλεονεξία, αἰσχρολογία,

ζηλοτυπία, θρασύτης, ὕψος, ἀλαζονεία. 2. διῶκται ἀγαθῶν, μισοῦντες ἀλήθειαν, ἀγαπῶντες ψεῦδος, οὐ γινώσκοντες μισθὸν δικαιοσύνης, οὐ κολλώμενοι ἀγαθῷ οὐδὲ κρίσει δικαίᾳ, ἀγρυπνοῦντες οὐκ εἰς τὸ ἀγαθὸν ἀλλ' εἰς τὸ πονηρόν· ὧν μακρὰν πραΰτης καὶ ὑπομονή, μάταια ἀγαπῶντες, διώκοντες ἀνταπόδομα, οὐκ ἐλεοῦντες πτωχόν, οὐ πονοῦντες ἐπὶ καταπονουμένῳ, οὐ γινώσκοντες τὸν ποιήσαντα αὐτούς, φονεῖς τέκνων, φθορεῖς πλάσματος θεοῦ, ἀποστρεφόμενοι τὸν ἐνδεόμενον, καταπονοῦντες τὸν θλιβόμενον, πλουσίων παράκλητοι, πενήτων ἄνομοι κριταί, πανθαμάρτητοι· ῥυσθείητε, τέκνα, ἀπὸ τούτων ἁπάντων.

CHAPTER SIX

1. Ὅρα, μή τίς σε πλανήσῃ ἀπὸ ταύτης τῆς ὁδοῦ τῆς διδαχῆς, ἐπεὶ παρεκτὸς θεοῦ σε διδάσκει. 2. εἰ μὲν γὰρ δύνασαι βαστάσαι ὅλον τὸν ζυγὸν τοῦ κυρίου, τέλειος ἔσῃ· εἰ δ' οὐ δύνασαι, ὃ δύνῃ, τοῦτο ποίει. 3. περὶ δὲ τῆς βρώσεως, ὃ δύνασαι βάστασον· ἀπὸ δὲ τοῦ εἰδωλοθύτου λίαν πρόσεχε· λατρεία γάρ ἐστι θεῶν νεκρῶν.

CHAPTER SEVEN

1. Περὶ δὲ τοῦ βαπτίσματος, οὕτω βαπτίσατε· ταῦτα πάντα προειπόντες, βαπτίσατε εἰς τὸ ὄνομα τοῦ πατρὸς καὶ τοῦ υἱοῦ καὶ τοῦ ἁγίου πνεύματος ἐν ὕδατι ζῶντι. 2. ἐὰν δὲ μὴ ἔχῃς ὕδωρ ζῶν, εἰς ἄλλο ὕδωρ βάπτισον· εἰ δ' οὐ δύνασαι ἐν ψυχρῷ, ἐν θερμῷ. 3. ἐὰν δὲ ἀμφότερα μὴ ἔχῃς, ἔκχεον εἰς τὴν κεφαλὴν τρὶς ὕδωρ εἰς ὄνομα πατρὸς καὶ υἱοῦ καὶ ἁγίου πνεύματος. 4. πρὸ δὲ τοῦ βαπτίσματος προνηστευσάτω ὁ βαπτίζων καὶ ὁ βαπτιζόμενος καὶ εἴ τινες ἄλλοι δύνανται· κελεύεις δὲ νηστεῦσαι τὸν βαπτιζόμενον πρὸ μιᾶς ἢ δύο.

CHAPTER EIGHT

1. Αἱ δὲ νηστεῖαι ὑμῶν μὴ ἔστωσαν μετὰ τῶν ὑποκριτῶν. νηστεύουσι γὰρ δευτέρᾳ σαββάτων καὶ πέμπτῃ· ὑμεῖς δὲ νηστεύσατε τετράδα καὶ παρασκευήν. 2. μηδὲ προσεύχεσθε ὡς οἱ ὑποκριταί, ἀλλ' ὡς ἐκέλευσεν ὁ κύριος ἐν τῷ εὐαγγελίῳ αὐτοῦ, οὕτω προσεύχεσθε· Πάτερ ἡμῶν ὁ ἐν τῷ οὐρανῷ, ἁγιασθήτω τὸ ὄνομά σου, ἐλθέτω ἡ βασιλεία σου, γενηθήτω τὸ θέλημά σου ὡς ἐν οὐρανῷ καὶ ἐπὶ γῆς· τὸν ἄρτον ἡμῶν τὸν ἐπιούσιον δὸς ἡμῖν σήμερον, καὶ ἄφες ἡμῖν τὴν ὀφειλὴν ἡμῶν, ὡς καὶ ἡμεῖς ἀφίεμεν τοῖς ὀφειλέταις ἡμῶν, καὶ μὴ εἰσενέγκῃς ἡμᾶς εἰς πειρασμόν, ἀλλὰ ῥῦσαι ἡμᾶς ἀπὸ τοῦ πονηροῦ· ὅτι σοῦ ἐστιν ἡ δύναμις καὶ ἡ δόξα εἰς τοὺς αἰῶνας. 3. τρὶς τῆς ἡμέρας οὕτω προσεύχεσθε.

CHAPTER NINE

1. Περὶ δὲ τῆς εὐχαριστίας, οὕτως εὐχαριστήσατε· 2. πρῶτον περὶ τοῦ ποτηρίου· Εὐχαριστοῦμέν σοι, πάτερ ἡμῶν, ὑπὲρ τῆς ἁγίας ἀμπέλου Δαυεὶδ τοῦ παιδός σου· ἧς ἐγνώρισας ἡμῖν

διὰ Ἰησοῦ τοῦ παιδός σου· σοὶ ἡ δόξα εἰς τοὺς αἰῶνας. 3. περὶ δὲ τοῦ κλάσματος· εὐχαριστοῦμέν σοι, πάτερ ἡμῶν, ὑπὲρ τῆς ζωῆς καὶ γνώσεως, ἧς ἐγνώρισας ἡμῖν διὰ Ἰησοῦ τοῦ παιδός σου. σοὶ ἡ δόξα εἰς τοὺς αἰῶνας. 4. ὥσπερ ἦν τοῦτο τὸ κλάσμα διεσκορπισμένον ἐπάνω τῶν ὀρέων καὶ συναχθὲν ἐγένετο ἕν, οὕτω συναχθήτω σου ἡ ἐκκλησία ἀπὸ τῶν περάτων τῆς γῆς εἰς τὴν σὴν βασιλείαν. ὅτι σοῦ ἐστιν ἡ δόξα καὶ ἡ δύναμις διὰ Ἰησοῦ Χριστοῦ εἰς τοὺς αἰῶνας. 5. μηδεὶς δὲ φαγέτω μηδὲ πιέτω ἀπὸ τῆς εὐχαριστίας ὑμῶν, ἀλλ᾽ οἱ βαπτισθέντες εἰς ὄνομα κυρίου· καὶ γὰρ περὶ τούτου εἴρηκεν ὁ κύριος· Μὴ δῶτε τὸ ἅγιον τοῖς κυσί.

CHAPTER TEN

1. Μετὰ δὲ τὸ ἐμπλησθῆναι οὕτως εὐχαριστήσατε· 2. Εὐχαριστοῦμέν σοι, πάτερ ἅγιε, ὑπὲρ τοῦ ἁγίου ὀνόματός σου, οὗ κατεσκήνωσας ἐν ταῖς καρδίαις ἡμῶν, καὶ ὑπὲρ τῆς γνώσεως καὶ πίστεως καὶ ἀθανασίας, ἧς ἐγνώρισας ἡμῖν διὰ Ἰησοῦ τοῦ παιδός σου· σοὶ ἡ δόξα εἰς τοὺς αἰῶνας. 3. σύ, δέσποτα παντοκράτορ, ἔκτισας τὰ πάντα ἕνεκεν τοῦ ὀνόματός σου, τροφήν τε καὶ ποτὸν ἔδωκας τοῖς ἀνθρώποις εἰς ἀπόλαυσιν, ἵνα σοι εὐχαριστήσωσιν, ἡμῖν δὲ ἐχαρίσω πνευματικὴν τροφὴν καὶ ποτὸν καὶ ζωὴν αἰώνιον διὰ τοῦ παιδός σου. 4. πρὸ πάντων εὐχαριστοῦμέν σοι, ὅτι δυνατὸς εἶ· σοὶ ἡ δόξα εἰς τοὺς αἰῶνας. 5. μνήσθητι, κύριε, τῆς ἐκκλησίας σου, τοῦ ῥύσασθαι αὐτὴν ἀπὸ παντὸς πονηροῦ καὶ τελειῶσαι αὐτὴν ἐν τῇ ἀγάπῃ σου, καὶ σύναξον αὐτὴν ἀπὸ τῶν τεσσάρων ἀνέμων, τὴν ἁγιασθεῖσαν, εἰς τὴν σὴν βασιλείαν, ἣν ἡτοίμασας αὐτῇ· ὅτι σοῦ ἐστιν ἡ δύναμις καὶ ἡ δόξα εἰς τοὺς αἰῶνας. 6. ἐλθέτω χάρις καὶ παρελθέτω ὁ κόσμος οὗτος. Ὡσαννὰ τῷ θεῷ Δαυείδ. εἴ τις ἅγιός ἐστιν, ἐρχέσθω· εἴ τις οὐκ ἔστι, μετανοείτω· μαρὰν ἀθά· ἀμήν. 7. τοῖς δὲ προφήταις ἐπιτρέπετε εὐχαριστεῖν ὅσα θέλουσιν.

CHAPTER ELEVEN

1. Ὃς ἂν οὖν ἐλθὼν διδάξῃ ὑμᾶς ταῦτα πάντα τὰ προειρημένα, δέξασθε αὐτόν· 2. ἐὰν δὲ αὐτὸς ὁ διδάσκων στραφεὶς διδάσκῃ ἄλλην διδαχὴν εἰς τὸ καταλῦσαι, μὴ αὐτοῦ ἀκούσητε· εἰς δὲ τὸ προσθεῖναι δικαιοσύνην καὶ γνῶσιν κυρίου, δέξασθε αὐτὸν ὡς κύριον. 3. Περὶ δὲ τῶν ἀποστόλων καὶ προφητῶν, κατὰ τὸ δόγμα τοῦ εὐαγγελίου οὕτω ποιήσατε. 4. πᾶς δὲ ἀπόστολος ἐρχόμενος πρὸς ὑμᾶς δεχθήτω ὡς κύριος· 5. οὐ μενεῖ δὲ εἰ μὴ ἡμέραν μίαν· ἐὰν δὲ ᾖ χρεία, καὶ τὴν ἄλλην· τρεῖς δὲ ἐὰν μείνῃ, ψευδοπροφήτης ἐστίν. 6. ἐξερχόμενος δὲ ὁ ἀπόστολος μηδὲν λαμβανέτω εἰ μὴ ἄρτον, ἕως οὗ αὐλισθῇ· ἐὰν δὲ ἀργύριον αἰτῇ, ψευδοπροφήτης ἐστί. 7. Καὶ πάντα προφήτην λαλοῦντα ἐν πνεύματι οὐ πειράσετε οὐδὲ διακρινεῖτε· πᾶσα γὰρ ἁμαρτία ἀφεθήσεται, αὕτη δὲ ἡ ἁμαρτία οὐκ ἀφεθήσεται. 8. οὐ πᾶς δὲ ὁ λαλῶν ἐν πνεύματι προφήτης ἐστίν, ἀλλ᾽ ἐὰν ἔχῃ τοὺς τρόπους κυρίου. ἀπὸ οὖν τῶν τρόπων γνωσθήσεται ὁ ψευδοπροφήτης καὶ ὁ προφήτης. 9. καὶ πᾶς προφήτης ὁρίζων τράπεζαν ἐν πνεύματι οὐ φάγεται ἀπ᾽ αὐτῆς, εἰ δὲ μήγε ψευδοπροφήτης ἐστί. 10. πᾶς δὲ προφήτης διδάσκων τὴν ἀλήθειαν, εἰ ἃ διδάσκει οὐ ποιεῖ, ψευδοπροφήτης ἐστί. 11. πᾶς δὲ προφήτης δεδοκιμασμένος, ἀληθινός, ποιῶν εἰς μυστήριον κοσμικὸν

ἐκκλησίας, μὴ διδάσκων δὲ ποιεῖν, ὅσα αὐτὸς ποιεῖ, οὐ κριθήσεται ἐφ' ὑμῶν· μετὰ θεοῦ γὰρ ἔχει τὴν κρίσιν· ὡσαύτως γὰρ ἐποίησαν καὶ οἱ ἀρχαῖοι προφῆται. 12. ὃς δ' ἂν εἴπῃ ἐν πνεύματι· δός μοι ἀργύρια ἢ ἕτερά τινα, οὐκ ἀκούσεσθε αὐτοῦ· ἐὰν δὲ περὶ ἄλλων ὑστερούντων εἴπῃ δοῦναι, μηδεὶς αὐτὸν κρινέτω.

CHAPTER TWELVE

1. Πᾶς δὲ ὁ ἐρχόμενος ἐν ὀνόματι κυρίου δεχθήτω· ἔπειτα δὲ δοκιμάσαντες αὐτὸν γνώσεσθε, σύνεσιν γὰρ ἔξετε δεξιὰν καὶ ἀριστεράν. 2. εἰ μὲν παρόδιός ἐστιν ὁ ἐρχόμενος, βοηθεῖτε αὐτῷ, ὅσον δύνασθε· οὐ μενεῖ δὲ πρὸς ὑμᾶς εἰ μὴ δύο ἢ τρεῖς ἡμέρας, ἐὰν ᾖ ἀνάγκη. 3. εἰ δὲ θέλει πρὸς ὑμᾶς καθῆσθαι, τεχνίτης ὤν, ἐργαζέσθω καὶ φαγέτω. 4. εἰ δὲ οὐκ ἔχει τέχνην, κατὰ τὴν σύνεσιν ὑμῶν προνοήσατε, πῶς μὴ ἀργὸς μεθ' ὑμῶν ζήσεται Χριστιανός. 5. εἰ δ' οὐ θέλει οὕτω ποιεῖν, χριστέμπορός ἐστι· προσέχετε ἀπὸ τῶν τοιούτων.

CHAPTER THIRTEEN

1. Πᾶς δὲ προφήτης ἀληθινὸς θέλων καθῆσθαι πρὸς ὑμᾶς ἄξιός ἐστι τῆς τροφῆς αὐτοῦ. 2. ὡσαύτως διδάσκαλος ἀληθινός ἐστιν ἄξιος καὶ αὐτὸς ὥσπερ ὁ ἐργάτης τῆς τροφῆς αὐτοῦ. 3. πᾶσαν οὖν ἀπαρχὴν γεννημάτων ληνοῦ καὶ ἅλωνος, βοῶν τε καὶ προβάτων λαβὼν δώσεις τὴν ἀπαρχὴν τοῖς προφήταις· αὐτοὶ γάρ εἰσιν οἱ ἀρχιερεῖς ὑμῶν. 4. ἐὰν δὲ μὴ ἔχητε προφήτην, δότε τοῖς πτωχοῖς. 5. ἐὰν σιτίαν ποιῇς, τὴν ἀπαρχὴν λαβὼν δὸς κατὰ τὴν ἐντολήν. 6. ὡσαύτως κεράμιον οἴνου ἢ ἐλαίου ἀνοίξας, τὴν ἀπαρχὴν λαβὼν δὸς τοῖς προφήταις· 7. ἀργυρίου δὲ καὶ ἱματισμοῦ καὶ παντὸς κτήματος λαβὼν τὴν ἀπαρχήν, ὡς ἄν σοι δόξῃ, δὸς κατὰ τὴν ἐντολήν.

CHAPTER FOURTEEN

1. Κατὰ κυριακὴν δὲ κυρίου συναχθέντες κλάσατε ἄρτον καὶ εὐχαριστήσατε, προεξομολο-γησάμενοι τὰ παραπτώματα ὑμῶν, ὅπως καθαρὰ ἡ θυσία ὑμῶν ᾖ. 2. πᾶς δὲ ἔχων τὴν ἀμφιβολίαν μετὰ τοῦ ἑταίρου αὐτοῦ μὴ συνελθέτω ὑμῖν, ἕως οὗ διαλλαγῶσιν, ἵνα μὴ κοινωθῇ ἡ θυσία ὑμῶν. 3. αὕτη γάρ ἐστιν ἡ ῥηθεῖσα ὑπὸ κυρίου· Ἐν παντὶ τόπῳ καὶ χρόνῳ προσφέρειν μοι θυσίαν καθαράν. ὅτι βασιλεὺς μέγας εἰμί, λέγει κύριος, καὶ τὸ ὄνομά μου θαυμαστὸν ἐν τοῖς ἔθνεσι.

CHAPTER FIFTEEN

1. Χειροτονήσατε οὖν ἑαυτοῖς ἐπισκόπους καὶ διακόνους ἀξίους τοῦ κυρίου, ἄνδρας πραεῖς καὶ ἀφιλαργύρους καὶ ἀληθεῖς καὶ δεδοκιμασμένους· ὑμῖν γὰρ λειτουργοῦσι καὶ αὐτοὶ τὴν λειτουρ-γίαν τῶν προφητῶν καὶ διδασκάλων. 2. μὴ οὖν ὑπερίδητε αὐτούς· αὐτοὶ γάρ εἰσιν οἱ τετιμημένοι ὑμῶν μετὰ τῶν προφητῶν καὶ διδασκάλων. 3. Ἐλέγχετε δὲ ἀλλήλους μὴ ἐν ὀργῇ, ἀλλ' ἐν εἰρήνῃ ὡς ἔχετε ἐν τῷ εὐαγγελίῳ· καὶ παντὶ ἀστοχοῦντι κατὰ τοῦ ἑτέρου μηδεὶς λαλείτω μηδὲ παρ'

ὑμῶν ἀκουέτω, ἕως οὗ μετανοήσῃ. 4. τὰς δὲ εὐχὰς ὑμῶν καὶ τὰς ἐλεημοσύνας καὶ πάσας τὰς πράξεις οὕτω ποιήσατε, ὡς ἔχετε ἐν τῷ εὐαγγελίῳ τοῦ κυρίου ἡμῶν.

CHAPTER SIXTEEN

1. Γρηγορεῖτε ὑπὲρ τῆς ζωῆς ὑμῶν· οἱ λύχνοι ὑμῶν μὴ σβεσθήτωσαν, καὶ αἱ ὀσφύες ὑμῶν μὴ ἐκλυέθωσαν, ἀλλὰ γίνεσθε ἕτοιμοι· οὐ γὰρ οἴδατε τὴν ὥραν, ἐν ᾗ ὁ κύριος ἡμῶν ἔρχεται. 2. πυκνῶς δὲ συναχθήσεσθε ζητοῦντες τὰ ἀνήκοντα ταῖς ψυχαῖς ὑμῶν· οὐ γὰρ ὠφελήσει ὑμᾶς ὁ πᾶς χρόνος τῆς πίστεως ὑμῶν, ἐὰν μὴ ἐν τῷ ἐσχάτῳ καιρῷ τελειωθῆτε. 3. ἐν γὰρ ταῖς ἐσχάταις ἡμέραις πληθυνθήσονται οἱ ψευδοπροφῆται καὶ οἱ φθορεῖς, καὶ στραφήσονται τὰ πρόβατα εἰς λύκους, καὶ ἡ ἀγάπη στραφήσεται εἰς μῖσος. 4. αὐξανούσης γὰρ τῆς ἀνομίας μισήσουσιν ἀλλήλους καὶ διώξουσι καὶ παραδώσουσι, καὶ τότε φανήσεται ὁ κοσμοπλανὴς ὡς υἱὸς θεοῦ, καὶ ποιήσει σημεῖα καὶ τέρατα, καὶ ἡ γῆ παραδοθήσεται εἰς χεῖρας αὐτοῦ, καὶ ποιήσει ἀθέμιτα, ἃ οὐδέποτε γέγονεν ἐξ αἰῶνος. 5. τότε ἥξει ἡ κτίσις τῶν ἀνθρώπων εἰς τὴν πύρωσιν τῆς δοκιμασίας, καὶ σκανδαλισθήσονται πολλοὶ καὶ ἀπολοῦνται, οἱ δὲ ὑπομείναντες ἐν τῇ πίστει αὐτῶν σωθήσονται ὑπ’ αὐτοῦ τοῦ καταθέματος. 6. καὶ τότε φανήσεται τὰ σημεῖα τῆς ἀληθείας· πρῶτον σημεῖον ἐκπετάσεως ἐν οὐρανῷ, εἶτα σημεῖον φωνῆς σάλπιγγος, καὶ τὸ τρίτον ἀνάστασις νεκρῶν. 7. οὐ πάντων δέ, ἀλλ’ ὡς ἐρρέθη· ἥξει ὁ κύριος καὶ πάντες οἱ ἅγιοι μετ’ αὐτοῦ. 8. τότε ὄψεται ὁ κόσμος τὸν κύριον ἐρχόμενον ἐπάνω τῶν νεφελῶν τοῦ οὐρανοῦ.